Workplace Etiquettes
for Success

Workplace Etiquettes for Success

Angie Klein

MURPHY & MOORE
www.murphy-moorepublishing.com

Workplace Etiquettes for Success
Angie Klein
ISBN: 978-1-63987-805-5 (Hardback)

⋈ MURPHY & MOORE

Murphy & Moore Publishing
1 Rockefeller Plaza,
New York City,
NY 10020, USA

Cataloging-in-Publication Data

Workplace etiquettes for success / Angie Klein.
    p. cm.
Includes bibliographical references and index.
ISBN 978-1-63987-805-5
1. Business etiquette. 2. Success in business. 3. Work ethic. 4. Work environment. I. Klein, Angie.
HF5389 .W67 2023
395.52--dc23

Table of Contents

Preface		**VII**
Chapter 1	**An Introduction to Workplace Etiquettes**	**1**
	• Etiquettes	1
	• Business Etiquette	1
	• How to Practice Office Etiquette	6
	• How to Behave at Work	16
	• How to Behave at a New Job	23
	• How to use Scheduling to Improve Punctuality	30
Chapter 2	**Workplace Communication Etiquettes**	**35**
	• How to Practice Cell Phone Etiquette	36
	• How to Answer the Phone at Work	41
	• How to Answer a Phone Call from Your Boss	46
	• How to Be Courteous with your Cell Phone at Work	53
	• How to Answer the Phone Politely	56
	• How to Be Polite on the Phone	62
	• How to Greet People on the Phone	68
	• How to use Proper Business Email Etiquette	75
	• How to Improve your Email Etiquette	79
	• How to Practice Business Meeting Etiquette	87
	• How to Practice Virtual Meetings Etiquette	88
	• How to Behave Professionally on Social Media	90
	• How to Practice Instant Messaging Etiquette	94
Chapter 3	**Hygiene Etiquettes at Workplace**	**101**
	• Cough and Sneeze Etiquette	101
	• How to Sneeze Properly	102
	• How to Sneeze Quietly	106
	• How to Practise Good Cough and Sneeze Etiquette	109
	• How to Avoid Common Hygiene Mistakes	110
	• How to use Restrooms at Work	119
Chapter 4	**Eating and Dining Etiquettes**	**124**
	• Eating Etiquette	124
	• How to Act during a Business Meal	125
	• Dining Etiquette in the Workplace	137
	• How to Maintain Business Lunch and Dinner Etiquette	139
	• How to use a Fork and Knife	145
	• How to use a Napkin with Proper Table Etiquette	152
	• How to Eat Soup Politely	154
	• How to Chew with your Mouth Closed	156
	• How to Avoid Spilling	158
	• How to React when you Spill Someone's Drink	160
	• How to Stir a Beverage Noiselessly	161

Chapter 5   **Dress Code for Workplace**   **164**
    • Corporate Dressing for Success at Workplace   164
    • How to Dress Professionally   165
    • How to Dress Business Casual   182

Permissions

Index

Preface

Workplace etiquettes are a code governing the expectations of professional and social conduct in a professional setting. There are no accepted universal work etiquettes. They may vary from one organization and environment to another. Work etiquettes encompass a range of considerations from body language and good behavior to the right use of technology. Effective communication and cooperation are other important facets of workplace etiquettes. Good business etiquettes are the key to building strong relationships in the workplace, which in turn can affect the success in a worker's professional life. This textbook is a compilation of topics that address some of the most vital aspects of workplace etiquettes that are crucial to success in the professional front. It studies, analyzes and upholds the pillars of professional ethics and its utmost significance in modern times. For all those who are desirous of professional success, this book can prove to be an essential guide.

A short introduction to every chapter is written below to provide an overview of the content of the book:

Chapter 1 - Workplace etiquette is a code, which governs social conduct in a workplace. This code is framed to protect and respect all individuals, the value of time and work processes. This chapter will serve as an introduction to workplace etiquettes. It thoroughly discusses office etiquette, the appropriate behavior at work, at a new job, etc.; **Chapter 2** - Appropriate business etiquette and manners are essential for building relations and communicating in the workplace. Being civil, showing empathy, a team-building attitude, presentability at work and using proper body language are some of the traits of a successful professional. This chapter describes the communication etiquettes required in a workplace environment, including the professional standards for answering the phone, writing a business email, communicating in a meeting, being professional on social media, etc.; **Chapter 3** - A workplace is a place with constant interactions among people. To ensure professionalism and goodwill, it is vital to practice good workplace hygiene. This chapter discusses in detail some cough and sneeze etiquettes for the workplace, the right use of washroom and the ways to avoid some common hygiene mistakes in the professional space; **Chapter 4** - It is imperative to exercise basic table manner while eating and dining. The right ways to chew, eating soup, using fork and knife, using a napkin, stirring a beverage, etc. are important eating and dining etiquettes. This chapter explores these etiquettes with respect to a professional setting; **Chapter 5** - Clothing regulations vary from one workplace to the other. Dress codes are generally set in the workplace for aesthetic recognition, or to look appropriate to their responsibilities. Dress codes may also regulate the use of jewelry and hats. This chapter examines professional dress code, business casual and corporate dressing.

I extend my sincere thanks to the publisher for considering me worthy of this task. Finally, I thank my family for being a source of support and help.

Angie Klein

An Introduction to Workplace Etiquettes

Workplace etiquette is a code, which governs social conduct in a workplace. This code is framed to protect and respect all individuals, the value of time and work processes. This chapter will serve as an introduction to workplace etiquettes. It thoroughly discusses office etiquette, the appropriate behavior at work, at a new job, etc.

Etiquettes

Etiquette is the complex network of rules that govern good behavior and our social and business interactions, is always evolving and changing as society changes. It reflects our cultural norms, generally accepted ethical codes, and the rules of various groups we belong to.

It helps us show respect and consideration to others and makes others glad that we are with them. Without proper manners and etiquette, the customs of polite society would soon disappear and we would act more like animals and less like people. Aggressiveness and an "every man for himself" attitude would take the lead.

Some people argue that etiquette no longer matters, that the rules for good behavior are old-fashioned and out of date. However, good behavior and manners are never out of style. Etiquette, like all other cultural behaviors, evolves to match the times. Without etiquette, members of society would show far too much impatience and disrespect for one another, which would lead to insults, dishonesty, cheating, road rage, fist fights, and a rash of other unfortunate incidents.

Etiquette is merely a set of guidelines for politeness and good manners, the kindnesses with which we should always treat each other.

Business Etiquette

"Business etiquette" is a term used to describe professional behavior in the workplace, and also in other settings in which business is conducted. Following business etiquette protocols serves as a means to establish individuals, companies and organizations as respectable and professional, which can create a sense of confidence for affiliates, customers and clients.

Types of Etiquette

While every business and professional organization sets its own standards for acceptable business etiquette practices, there are some standard behaviors and best practices companies and business professionals should be aware of. Business etiquette examples include:

Personal Interactions

The ways in which people in a business personally interact with customers, vendors, business associates, and even with each other, creates a perception of the values of the organization. For example, if you walked into an office and the receptionist ignored you or said, "What do you want?" in an unfriendly tone, would you feel welcome and respected? Most likely not. Etiquette dictates that employees use a professional greeting style, with an eye toward making others feel important, appreciated and valued. This also extends to common niceties such as offering your hand to others, making eye contact and speaking without without interrupting others. Best practices in this area should be in employee handbooks, and should be discussed with new hires, as part of orientation or onboarding.

Language Use

Even in a laid-back environment, language that staffers use reflects on the business. Etiquette and internal protocols should dictate how others are addressed. For example, are people refereed to by first or last name. Or, are they addressed with honorific titles. In most professional settings, slang is discouraged, and foul language is off-limits. Even jokes and teasing are a breach of etiquette protocols in most business environments. Language practices are not limited to personal internal conversation, but also as to how employees speak with customers in-person and by phone. In businesses that have an international workforce or clientele, additional diligence is required to ensure that language protocols are in place and followed.

Hospitality Practices

Etiquette is about making others comfortable. This might mean offering beverages to guests, validating parking passes and ensuring adequate seating and work space, as necessary. If a business is involved with making travel arrangements, then etiquette demands that employees understand any special accommodation needs that they make arrangements for travel costs, shuttles, car rental and lodging. If a per diem or an expense reimbursement is offered, etiquette practices encourage rapid attention to processing payments.

Dress Code

The way you dress in a business environment reveals your professionalism, and etiquette dictates specific attire for different functions. Business attire is expected in professional work environments, with upscale business dress worn for high-level meetings and presentations. Overly casual clothing, ill-fitting, unpressed, dirty or revealing clothing, or garish accessories break etiquette. As exceptions to this rule, individuals employed in fields where they perform manual labor or where uniforms are worn, attention to the specific dress code of that industry is appropriate.

Written Communications

Much like the language spoken in a business, the ways in which written communications are handled require a nod toward good etiquette practices. For example, address letters and emails following standard business letter writing formats, using, "Ms.," "Mr." or "Dr." Use formal language and grammatically correct sentence structure, and a sign-off that reads, "regards," or "sincerely." Make note of those copied on correspondence and use the professional courtesy of ensuring all necessary information is included before sending.

Email Etiquette

While email can be fast and informal, etiquette dictates a more professional approach with business emails. Use complete sentences, reference attachments, make subject lines relevant and include signature blocks with full contact information. Avoid unnecessarily CC-ing multiple parties, and use caution when forwarding materials that might be sensitive. Remember, business email is just that - don't use it for jokes, personal correspondence, spam or sharing political opinions.

Telephone Practices

Etiquette requires formal telephone skills as well. For example, introduce yourself and your company and ask for the person you're calling to speak with. If that person isn't available, leave a detailed message including your phone numbers and email contact information. Keep in mind that with so many spam calls coming from unidentified or unfamiliar numbers, many people will screen or allow calls to go to voicemail, so identification is key to ensuring your messages get through. Etiquette also dictates that you don't take or place calls in noisy locations or where you're likely to lose cell service.

Video and Teleconference Practices

If you're not speaking with someone face-to-face or one-on-one, etiquette has a few rules for ensuring that everyone is seen, heard and understood in group settings, or when communication may be challenging. For example, in a teleconference, take turns speaking, and introduce yourself before you speak or respond. When videoconferencing, pick a quiet location, with no distractions in the background. Set the cameras so that everyone in a group is visible, and speak clearly.

Meeting Etiquette

When it comes to business meeting etiquette, it's all about common courtesy and manners. Arrive on time, stay on point with the agenda or moderator's direction, take turns speaking and don't over-talk or interrupt. Be prepared for meetings as a way to demonstrate your respect for others' time. Don't allow yourself to be distracted, even if agenda items don't apply directly to you or your work. Business etiquette requires undivided attention. If you are using an electronic device to take notes, make it clear that's what you're using the device for.

Meal Etiquette

Business meals can sometimes feel awkward, particularly if you're dining with strangers, or you're trying to eat and conduct business at the same time. Following simple forms of dining etiquette can make things go smoothly. Examples:

1. If you're the host, make reservations, confirm the meal/meeting, time and location with your guests, and arrive early. Let your host or server know that the bill is to be brought to

you at the end of the meal. Encourage guests to order anything they would like, and if there is hesitation, take the lead by ordering something from the upper price end of the menu. Be kind and generous with your wait staff.

2. If you're the guest, arrive on time, but if your host hasn't arrived, wait for your host before being seated. Allow the host to direct which comes first - food or business talk. Order from the middle of the menu's price range, and don't speak with your mouth full. All parties should use caution when ordering alcohol. Always wait until everyone's food has arrived, before you start eating, and never ask for a to-go box.

When people bring food to work to share, wait until everyone has had an opportunity to sample the goods before taking a second helping. If you bring food, indicate any particular allergens it may contain, such as nuts or gluten. If you don't care to participate in potluck-style shared meals at work, that's fine - but business etiquette states that if you don't bring something to share, you don't eat what others have brought. It should go without saying that you should never help yourself to food, that isn't yours, from the shared company lunchroom or refrigerator.

Tip

- If you're at a business cocktail party and you're nursing a drink, it is best to wipe your hands after eating finger foods, and remember that the purpose of the meeting is more business than bar-scene socializing.

Electronics Etiquette

Everyone is attached to a phone or an electronic device these days, but there are still etiquette policies to follow in a business setting.

- Turn off your phone during meetings and presentations.

- Don't take calls during business conversations, unless it's absolutely necessary; excuse yourself if you must take the call.

- Refrain from checking email, sending texts - or worse - playing games or surfing the internet or social media while in a business setting.

- Use good judgment when having business conversations on phones outside the office, particularly in public areas - protect confidential or sensitive information from being overheard.

Think twice before taking or placing a call while driving. Not only is this dangerous to you and to other drivers and pedestrians, but you're unlikely to be able to give the conversation your undivided attention. You may appear rude, distracted or unprepared - all breaches of business etiquette. States have specific laws relating to what you can and cannot do with a cell phone while driving. Often, stiff penalties apply. States vary in their laws, so it is best to consult your state's drive registry for laws specific to your state.

Tip

- Just because your colleagues, managers and direct reports - and even your clients - likely have their phones on them at all times, doesn't mean you should call, text or email them during off-hours, unless it's absolutely necessary.

Shared Space Etiquette

When people work in close quarters with shared work space, etiquette requires certain collective behaviors for maximum productivity and minimal discourse.

Tips to this end include:

- Have respect for shared equipment and space. Replace the paper in empty printer trays, make a new pot of coffee when you take the last cup, and clean up any messes in shared work spaces.

- Speak quietly when in close quarters, to maintain confidential conversations and also so you don't disrupting others' work.

- Respect closed doors and people talking on phones.

- Don't dominate work time with personal discussions.

- Keep your own space tidy, clean and odor-free; remember, it's not only noxious odors such as pungent food or potpourri that's distasteful - too much perfume or cologne can also invade others' senses.

Tip

- Practice good personal hygiene and perform grooming habits privately in bathrooms, not at your desk or in the open, where others can see you.

Pay Attention

Etiquette is often a matter of paying attention to others, in a genuine way. This means listening intently during conversations, asking questions, providing meaningful feedback and generally taking an interest in what the other person is saying or doing. This also holds true when attending seminars, listening to internal presentations and meeting with clients. Others know when you're only phoning it in and that you're not genuinely interested. Make an effort to engage with others, and you may find that you have better-than-expected results, all while also establishing worthwhile relationships.

Professional Courtesies

Etiquette includes observation of certain types of professional courtesies. These include:

- Introducing others in a professional setting, using full names and titles.

- Following up as promised, on delivery of work product, referrals, returned phone calls and emails.

- Respecting the time of others, including being on time and meeting deadlines.

The importance of business etiquette cannot be overstated, because business etiquette demands kindly behavior toward one another. This means that you avoid gossip, you don't speak poorly about another, put down your colleagues or attempt to strong-arm business associates or customers into deals that benefit you but that may be detrimental to them. Etiquette in business means that you are reliable, dependable and that you ensure that others feel confident and at-ease when doing business with you.

Importance of Business Etiquette

Just as people make first impressions between one another, businesses and their employees also create first impressions. Practicing business etiquette helps create a positive impression, which is a way to demonstrate respect for others and also to instill a sense of pride in the company. Failure to follow common business etiquette practices can dissuade customers and businesses from wanting a relationship with your organization, since poor etiquette practices can signal that your organization may be unprofessional. By association, uncouth behaviors and practices can also hint at a less-than-stellar product or service.

How to Practice Office Etiquette

Good workplace manners are the glue that hold the happiest companies together. With good office etiquette, you'll feel comfortable around your coworkers and make a great impression on your supervisor. Your workplace will feel like a second home in no time.

Method 1. Practicing Personal Workplace Habits

1. Dress appropriately. Every workplace has a slightly different dress code, but in general, avoid wearing clothes that are revealing, overly casual or too loose or tight. If you're not sure what your office's dress code is, ask a friendly coworker or your boss, and observe what others wear. It may be acceptable to wear nice jeans, or you may want to stick to slacks, button-down shirts and blouses, and skirts. Determine what your dress code is and stick to it.

- You can still buy nice work clothes if you're on a budget by mixing and matching coordinating styles and buying at off-the-rack stores.

2. Avoid overpowering perfume or cologne. You and your coworkers are probably in close quarters so keep your office scent subtle. You don't want it to irritate anyone's nose or even give them an allergic reaction. If you choose to wear a scent, dab only small amounts on your pulse points, like your wrists, and not on your clothing.

3. Stay home when you're sick. Use up those sick days when you have them. You may feel guilty about losing a day of work, but taking the day off will help you recover faster and prevent you from exposing the rest of the office to your illness.

- Even if you're not contagious, your constant coughing or nose-blowing could distract your coworkers, meaning that the whole office is unproductive and annoyed. Save everyone the trouble, grab some medicine and take the day off.

4. Be polite over email. Keep your emails polite, concise and to the point. Avoid discussing private

matters, like a client's financial information, and speaking badly of any of your coworkers. With a simple click of the "Forward" button, your email can be shared with the whole company, so make sure everything in it is polite and professional.

- Keep your language workplace appropriate. Save the emojis and exclamation points for texts with friends.

5. Keep your social media appropriate. Even if you have your social media set to private, your co-workers and even your boss will find a way to see it if they want to. Before you post, ask yourself, "Is this something I don't mind my boss seeing? Is posting this worth sacrificing the respect of my employer, or losing my job?" Avoid overly raunchy posts or pictures with drugs or alcohol, especially if you're under the legal drinking age.

6. Eat in the lunchroom or outside. This is especially important if you're eating strong-smelling foods. It's fine to heat up your leftover fish in the microwave, but find a place to eat it where it won't disturb your coworkers. If it's a nice day, sit outside. Otherwise, head for the lunchroom or an empty conference room.

- Even the sound of chewing, crunching or slurping can be annoying to some noise-sensitive coworkers. Respect their preferences and enjoy your meal outside the office.

7. Don't take other people's food from the communal lunch area. It can be tough to tell when food is communal or personal, especially if it's in an open container or is sitting in the middle of the fridge. Err on the side of caution; if it's not clearly marked as something that's free for the taking, leave it alone. There's no faster way to ruin a coworker's day than by eating their lunch.

- Pack your own lunch in a bag or container and attach a sticky note with your name on it to avoid confusion.

- If you do accidentally take someone else's food, be honest and own up to it. Say, "I'm so sorry that I ate your salad. I thought it was someone's leftovers they were giving away. Let me go buy you another one."

8. Avoid office gossip. Cubicle walls are thin and if you talk badly about a coworker, chances are it will find its way back to them, no matter how large your office is. If you're frustrated with your boss and need to vent, do so outside of work.

- If it coworkers invite you to gossip, say, "I've got to get back to my desk, I'm so swamped right now."

- As much as you dislike your boss or coworker now, it'll be much worse if word gets back to them that you were talking about them behind their backs.

Method 2. Respecting Cubicle Space

1. Take phone conversations in a private room. This shows that you respect your coworkers' working environment and don't want to distract them with your conversations, whether personal or work-related. Cubicle walls are pretty thin, so if you think your conversation will last more than a minute or two, it's best to take it outside.

2. Decorate your cubicle simply and tastefully. A neat cubicle shows your boss and coworkers that you respect your work and your working environment. Keeping your space clean, organized, and decorated will make it feel welcoming and friendly. Hang up pictures of your family or good friends.

- Steer clear of anything political as well as offensive pictures, posters, or slogans.

- If you're not sure if something is appropriate or not, ask yourself if you'd be comfortable with the president of the company seeing it in your cubicle. If the answer is no, take it down and use it to decorate your home instead.

3. "Knock" before you talk. Be respectful of your coworkers' time. If you need to talk with them

and don't have a scheduled meeting, knock on the side of their cubicle before you start to speak, as they may be deep in concentration, or even on the phone. When they look up, say, "Do you have a second to chat?" If they're busy, make plans to talk later, or ask them to come by your cubicle when they're free.

- Avoid lingering too long at a coworker's desk, especially if they seem busy. They'd love to hear about your weekend plans at lunch, but not when they're in the middle of an important email.

4. Leave a note if a coworker is busy or away from their desk. Write down what you want to talk about on a sticky note and put it on the desk where your coworker will see it, but not right in front of their nose if they're sitting there. Ask them to swing by your cubicle when they have a second.

- If the coworker is clearly on a call, don't distract them by whispering or using your hands to communicate. Be patient and leave a note or come back later when they're off the call.

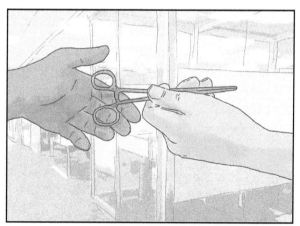

5. Ask before you borrow any items. Most offices have a communal pool of the usual office supplies, like staples, post-it notes, pens, and notepads. If you need a tool that only your coworker has, be sure to ask before you bring it back to your desk.

- If you need an item immediately, leave a note on their desk saying, "Borrowed the hole-punch for a couple minutes. I'll return as soon as I'm done." Sign your name so they know who to find if their hole-punch never makes it back.

6. Use your cubicle for working, not personal time. It looks unprofessional if you use your cubicle as a dressing room or a place for personal grooming, like doing your makeup or flossing your teeth. Take your toothbrush and nail clippers to the bathroom and touch up your makeup without your cubicle-mates giving you weird looks--it'll be more comfortable that way anyways.

Method 3. Using Good Etiquette in an Open Office

1. Respect your coworkers' space. This is even more important in an open office environment where there's not much separating you from your coworkers. Don't let your paper or work items spill onto someone else's space and make sure to ask before using something on someone else's desk, even if it's just a stapler or a piece of paper.

2. Be neat and limit personal items to your space. When your desk is out in the open or even shared with other coworkers, it's even more important to keep it tidy, since it could affect your coworkers'

ability to focus. Limit yourself to only one or two non-work related pictures or items. Keep your paperwork in neat piles or organized into folders.

3. Be tolerant of other personalities. An open-office space will bring you in close contact with lots of other personalities, which is great for fostering new ideas and getting to know lots of people. On the flipside, it can be stressful to be at the same desk all day with a coworker you don't like. Keep an open mind and concentrate on learning from other people's perspectives, even if you don't always agree with them.

4. Keep noise to a minimum. Take phone calls outside or in a conference room, especially personal ones or conversations you think could last for a while. Listen to music with headphones, never out loud, and avoid yelling across the room or talking loudly. It can be fun to work in a big room with all your coworkers, but you don't want to make the environment so loud that no one can focus and get their work done.

5. Ask your coworkers if they have a second before you start talking. It's all too easy to disrupt

coworkers' workflow when you're sitting right across from them. To avoid pestering someone who's in deep concentration, say quietly, "Hey, do you have a second to talk about this project?" That way, they can finish up what they're working on before they start meeting with you.

- If your office uses an online messaging service, you could ping them that way as well, or leave a post-it note on their desk if they seem particularly busy.

6. Keep casual or personal conversations to a minimum. A benefit of an open office workspace is being able to strike up casual conversations with the coworkers around you. If you chat for too long, though, other people will get distracted--and probably a bit annoyed. Save longer conversations for lunchtime or after work.

Method 4. Being Polite during Meetings

1. Show up on time. Your coworkers and supervisors won't be happy if they have to hold up a whole meeting because you got lost on the way to the conference room, or needed a drink of water. Keep your meetings organized on a calendar and stop working ten minutes before so you can gather all the materials you'll need. Confirm that you know where the meeting is and take a quick bathroom break before you head in.

2. Silence your cell phone, or turn it off. A cell phone ringing in the middle of a meeting is even worse than one going off in a movie theater. Make sure yours is on silent or turned off before the meeting starts, or leave it in a locked drawer at your desk to avoid the distraction altogether.

3. Give the speaker your full attention. Close your laptop and set aside your phone--no multi-tasking here. Listen attentively and take notes on a notepad if it helps you pay attention. Active listening and participation in a meeting is polite and shows that you care about the information. When it's your turn to present or lead a meeting, people will return the favor.

4. Hold meetings in a conference room, not your desk. If you're meeting with two or more people, head for a conference room or break area so you won't distract those working around you. You could even head outside for a walking meeting, or to talk over lunch.

5. End meetings on time. Keeping your meetings efficient and productive will show that you respect your coworkers' time, getting them out on time and freeing up the conference room for the next group to get started. Remember, your coworkers are just as busy as you are.

How to Behave at Work

Your attitude is just as important as your skills and abilities. From offices to restaurants, learning to navigate any new job requires a unique mixture of people skills and dedication. You can learn to make a good impression on your first day, and turn that good impression into a good reputation into the future.

Part 1. Starting a New Job

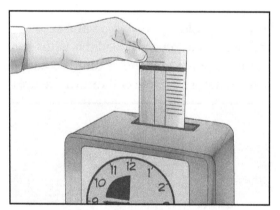

1. Get there early. On your first day, it's important to make a good impression and to show up on time. Make sure you're there early enough to get fully prepared and changed, if necessary, to start your shift. Be there ready to go 10-15 minutes before your shift starts. Budget your time well in advance, giving yourself an extra 30-40 minutes as a buffer for things like traffic, getting lost, and finding parking.

- If you have to take public transportation, or your new workplace is somewhere you're unfamiliar with, take the trip a few days ahead of time to make sure you know exactly how long it will take, and where it is.

- Don't stay beyond the time you're scheduled. Leaving late may indicate that you aren't able to budget your time effectively. Impress your employer by arriving early enough to prepare for the day, then leave when you're finished.

2. Listen and apply what you hear. You won't be expected to excel right away at most jobs, and most employers know that there will be a learning curve with new hires. So, don't worry so much about making mistakes and messing up your first day, but focus on learning as much as possible and listening closely to make sure you don't miss things.

- Be conscious of your learning style. If you are a hands-on learner, for example, ask the person training you to walk you through a task rather than having you watch them.

- Take a notepad or notebook with you so that you can take down important points during your training. Ask questions and be sure to jot down the answers.

- Make it your goal to only make a mistake once. If your boss tells you how to do something, listen and remember so you won't have to ask again.

3. Don't be afraid to ask questions. Lots of new employees will be too sheepish to ask questions, and will blunder into doing things incorrectly. Know enough to know when you need help. There's no shame in asking for help, especially on your first day. It'll be better to have it explained once and be sure you'll do it right than to try to guess and get exposed later.

4. Try to anticipate what needs to happen next. The process of every workplace is very different. Even if you're skilled and talented, it takes some time to figure out what needs to happen, and in what order. The best way to stand out on your first day as a good worker is to try to analyze the situation and figure out what needs to happen next.

- At some jobs, your first day can involve a lot of standing around and watching. Jump in when you see an opening. If you see another employee carrying a big stack of bags from one place to another, you don't need to be told that you could help out.

- At some jobs, you'll need to ask instead of just acting. If you're starting at a kitchen and finish up with some dishes, it might seem obvious that they'll go to the dishwasher, but there may be some other process. Ask.

5. Clean up without being asked. One thing that's consistent at every workplace is cleanliness and safety. Straightening up doesn't usually need to be coached. Look out for things you can organize, or ways that you can clean up to make the workplace much easier.

- If you work in an office, change out the coffee filter and make a fresh pot. Clean up the cups and spoons and throw away the refuse. Take the trash to the bin. Help straighten up other public areas if they need straightening.

- If you work in a kitchen or a restaurant, keep an eye out for obstacles that someone may trip over, or help clean up dishes in the back. Take a turn at the sink if you need to. try to find a way to stay busy.

6. Just be yourself. It's not what you know, how talented you are, or even what you do on the first day that will make it a success. It's your attitude and behavior. Your employer hired you because there was something about your combination of skills and personality that will benefit your workplace. Have faith in your ability to succeed as yourself, and don't think you need to be someone you're not.

- You don't have to act like your coworkers act, for good or for worse. It takes time for people to adjust to a new person in the workplace, so give your co-workers time to adjust to your personality rather than changing your behavior to match theirs.

Part 2. Being a Good Worker

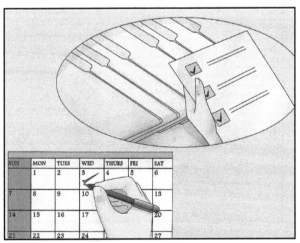

1. Set short-term work goals. Being a good employee involves going above and beyond the call of duty. Try to be the best employee that you can be by setting personal goals in the short term to help yourself stand out. After a few days of work, try to identify the things you need to work on the most and make it your goal to get where you want to be.

- If you're working in a kitchen, make it your goal to have all the sandwich recipes memorized by the end of the month, so you don't have to consult your cheat sheet. Or make it your goal to get your plate time down to that of the other employees.

- Focus more on the quality of your work and less on your efficiency in your first couple of weeks. Make every sandwich well before you worry about making it quickly. Worry about getting faster and producing more as you go on.

2. Be willing and realistic about what you can do. Good employees are volunteers, willing to take on extra responsibilities and tasks when asked. If you want to cultivate a reputation as a reliable employee, then be willing to do things that need to be done.

- It's also important to know your limits. If you've already got 10 things to do before you leave today, don't volunteer to do one more thing that's going to take several hours. Budget your time effectively.

- Be cautious when you need to be too. If a fellow employee asks you to do something you're not sure about, it may be more helpful to think up an alternative plan. Be tactful and defer to your boss for help, if necessary.

3. Just do your work, don't do anyone else's. A good employee is committed to doing their job well without trying to manage the way others work. When you're at work, stay focused on doing what you need to do to the best of your abilities. Don't spend time getting into other people's work unless they specifically ask for your advice or help. Stand out by getting everything done that you need to do.

- Try to avoid workplace gossip. It's easy to group into little work cliques that can distract you from your responsibilities. Just focus on doing your work, not how well other people do their work.

4. Be active. If you see debris littering the floor of your workplace, don't walk around it, then inform your boss that someone needs to do a little picking up. Just pick it up yourself. Do things for the sake of creating a better work environment, not looking like you're a better employee.

5. Bring something extra to the table. Do your work well and complete it, then look for ways you can do a little extra to help the company you work for reaching its goals. Good employees come to the table with creative ideas for improvements and efficiency tactics to help make your workplace a better place.

- Try to come up with a few creative ideas each couple of months, then keep them on hand in case they come in handy. Grab five minutes to chat about your idea in private with your boss, instead of bringing it up at a big group meeting.

Part 3. Having the Right Attitude

1. Establish long-term work goals. Where do you want to be in five years? Ten? How can this job help you get there? Set clear and achievable goals for yourself at your job, and work toward them

each week. Knowing how your work relates to your ultimate goals in life will give you self-assurance and provide motivation for you to advance your company and yourself.

- Try to keep a list of what you're working toward, to help get you through the weeks. What you're doing right now might not seem that important, but how is this helping you get what you want? How is this moving you up the ladder?

- The ultimate goals of the company you work for are also important, and should be kept at the front of your mind.

2. Speak well of other employees. Employers appreciate employees who support other good workers. When you work hard and consistently help further your company's goals, you become a trusted voice. Use your voice to help others who are worthy of praise and advancement.

- If other employees mock or criticize a fellow employee, don't participate. It can be easy to form snarky cliques at work, but it can create a toxic work culture. Don't be a part of it.

- If you gossip, lie, or cheat in order to gain position in the company, you may gain ground in the short term, but lose it in the long term as you built up bad relationships with other employees. Allow your employer to evaluate your work and skills, and determine where you fit best in the company.

3. Get invested in what you're doing. Employers value employees who take pride in what they're doing. If you're doing something you're really passionate about, that's easy. But if you're working a job for the wage, it can be a little more difficult to find that passion. Find some way to get more invested in what you're doing, to let your passion shine through.

- Stay focused now what this job affords you, and remind yourself that succeeding in this job makes all those things easier. If you're working to feed your family, or to pay your way through college, remind yourself that what you do at work has a direct impact on those parts of your life.

4. Treat everyone you encounter with dignity and respect. While some people can be very difficult to interact with in the workplace, when you treat them poorly you should remember that you are negatively affecting your career opportunities with the company. Your co-workers were as carefully selected as you were, so showing contempt for and disrespect for any co-worker you encounter shows a disregard for the intellect of your employer.

How to Behave at a New Job

Part 1. Being Successful Your First Day

1. Prepare for your first day at work. Starting on the right foot is essential. People will form lasting impressions of you as early as the first day. You want to do your homework and make ample preparation. Without preparation, you may run into difficulties and find yourself unnecessarily aggravated or irritable. Being short or snapping at another co-worker is a terrible way to start a relationship.

- Make sure to either bring or ask for a notebook to begin taking notes early in the day. Bringing one from home shows initiative. Don't be the new employee who doesn't write anything down.

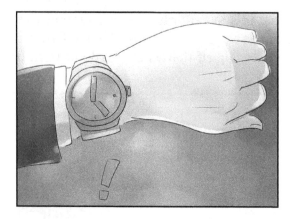

2. Arrive early and ready to work. Plan to be there at least 15 minutes early. Report directly to your boss or human resources contact.

- If you don't know where to go, kindly let another employee know this is your first day and ask them for directions. They had a first day too so they will understand.

3. Turn your cell phone off. Until you know the rules, assume that using your cell phone during business hours is grounds for immediate termination (this assumption is not far from reality). The first day is all about first impressions. Any cell phone interruption signals a lack of professionalism.

4. Prepare to be civil and cordial.Most of the bad workplace behaviors come from a lack of respect for others. While your co-workers function in a variety of roles at work, they are still people with feelings. Being nice and leaving hand written Thank You's builds positive working relationships.

- Prepare to avoid joking or discussing race, gender, age, sexual orientation, or religion. These are sensitive issues for most people. Even if you are comfortable discussing these topics, many other people may feel uncomfortable if you discuss them openly.

- Resist the temptation to ask or pry into people's personal lives. If your curiosity is tickled, ask yourself if the answer is work-related? If not, its best to not ask.

- Drive carefully in the parking lot and don't be rude to others as you are rushing to clock in or out on time. Even if you are not on the clock, the people you are speeding past and bumping into are still your co-workers.

5. Introduce yourself to others with a smile. Smile and take time to introduce yourself in the elevator or to colleagues at the desks across from yours. This small step will help you start developing a relationship with co-workers and let them know you're part of the team.

- As you introduce yourself to others, make an effort to remember their names and positions. Write names and positions in your notebook to memorize. If necessary, note memorable physical features or personal characteristics to help you match faces with names. Quickly learning names shows others you value them.

6. Ask questions as they arise. You will not know how to do everything nor will you understand the processes on the first day. When you run into a problem, ask someone promptly. The first day it is better to ask and verify than to do something wrong. Since it is your first day, you have a license to ask too many questions. Remember to write down the response in your notebook for future reference.

- If someone is going through a procedure too fast for you to write, ask them to slow down. This may seem rude, but they will appreciate it it. If you write everything down properly, they won't have to repeat themselves later.

- When you've finished a set of instructions, repeat the process back to your instructor. This gives them a chance to ensure you have documented the process properly. They may also emphasize certain points you will want to highlight.

7. Follow directions closely and precisely. You may know how to do something already, but follow their directions first. Ask before deviating from their process. There may be critical and clear reasons why their methods are different.

- ISO-9001 and other standards have strict rules you may not anticipate. Using a pencil, white-out, or a colored ink pen could land you in hot water with your boss. Even benign changes to procedures can negatively impact your performance.

- If you are given a computer, do not attempt to view webpages or download files without permission. This includes checking your personal email or downloading backgrounds. This may seem benign but may cause you to get in trouble with the computer services department.

Part 2. Finishing the First Month

1. Review and expand your notes continuously. After the first day you are expected to remember what you've been repeatedly told. Anytime you have an issue, review your notebook first. Asking for directions only if necessary. This helps show you are capable of working independently. The sooner you can show this, the more respect you will earn from your co-workers.

2. Demonstrate consistently appropriate work behavior. Continue to show up to work early, dressed appropriate, and ready to work. The first month people develop clear expectations about you. This will influence how they treat you as a co-worker.

- If you are late or make a business dress faux pas, take responsibility for your mistake. Traffic may have been bad, but you could have accounted for it. Making excuses for your temporary lack of etiquette show immaturity.

3. Read all employment information. Anything your boss or human resources department hands you to read over, do so promptly. Ask questions where you do not understand. Make notes of any rules you think will be difficult to remember or that you think you might break accidentally.

- For example, at most jobs, discussing pay is considered "unethical" and may be grounds for termination. Discussing politics and religion may also get you in trouble even if you do so off-the-clock.

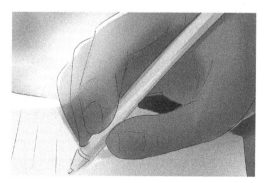

4. Complete any forms promptly. Many forms must be completed within the first week or month

of employment. These include tax and health insurance enrollment forms such as a W-2. You may need to ask your human resources contact how to appropriately fill out these forms.

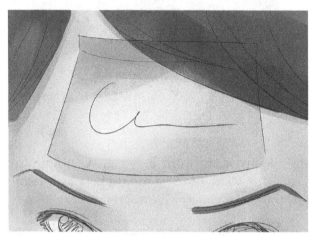

5. Memorize people's names and relationships. Beyond just your boss and co-workers, you need to learn the names and relationships of people throughout the company. People who you will meet face-to-face and department heads are particularly important.

- If you are feeling overwhelmed learning people's names and positions, trying drawing a diagram of each department with the department head at the top and everyone under them below. As you learn people's positions, you can write them down and orient them vertically according to their role.

6. Stay confident and relax. It's a new job and there's a lot to learn, but don't let it intimidate you. Remember you earned that job due to your experience and let your workplace attitude display that confidence and experience. If you get frustrated or overwhelmed, take a deep breath and try again. Let your new bosses see that you work well in new situations and under pressure.

- No matter how many notes you write you will still mess up. When corrected, say "thank you" and look over your notes for errors. Do not blame another co-worker even if you believe their instructions were incomplete. Review your updated instructions with the person correcting you.

7. Accept lunch invitations if offered. Even if you brought your lunch, your lunch break is more than food. Its about being social with co-workers and bosses. Being invited to lunch signals interest. This gives you an opportunity to develop a deeper, better relationship with this person.

8. Stay in business mode. Whether you are at lunch with a co-worker or at home posting on social media you shouldn't relax too much. Whenever work is involved, stay in a professional mindset. Subtle or abrupt changes to your level of professional courtesy may be construed as a lack of respect.

9. Work as a team player. You're a new employee, but you're part of a team. Ask questions and accept criticism with a smile.

- When you've completed your assigned tasks, ask your manager or superior what you can be doing to help the team. Don't be afraid to ask questions if you're asked to participate in a team or group function. Co-workers will be more likely to help you out and answer your questions if you establish yourself as a team player.

- Engage your new co-workers in conversation when they welcome you to the team, but stay neutral in your opinions about them. You're just as likely to get welcomed into the office fantasy football pool as you are to get targeted by the office gossip, so remain objective until you know whose welcome is genuine.

- Do not be quick to complain about your work even if asked what you do not like about the job so far. Focus on how you can improve your own job performance.

How to use Scheduling to Improve Punctuality

If you find that you are always late or running late and have problems with being on time for work and appointments, it could be that you need a more well thought out daily schedule. Find out how to use scheduling to improve punctuality and make your life run more smoothly.

Steps

1. Set aside time to set realistic goals for your professional and personal life. This includes all aspects, from career advancement to family life to personal health and satisfaction. If you are always late, working to improve being on time should be one of your goals.

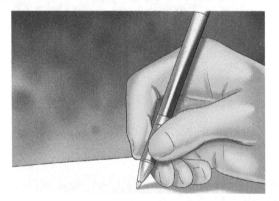

2. Use your list of goals to create a to-do list. Break the list down into years, months and weeks to determine what has to be done when.

3. Set up a scheduling program. What you use depends on your personal preferences. Use a written daily planner or an electronic schedule program. Electronic and computer based programs include PDAs, Microsoft Outlook, spreadsheets and software scheduling programs. You may need to experiment with a few methods before you find the right one for you that makes it easy to learn how to use scheduling to improve punctuality.

4. Set the time that you have available in the scheduling program. Block out time for essential tasks, like work and urgent obligations.

5. Allow time in the schedule for interruptions and preparation. This includes tasks like getting ready for work, finding appointment locations, and getting directions. Be sure to allow a little more time that you think you will need. Schedule times for social activities and phone calls instead of letting them interrupt your work.

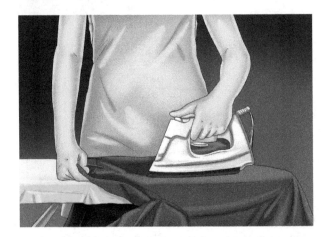

6. Leave time in the schedule for advanced preparation. Some preparation tasks should be done the day or night before an appointment, like laying out clothes and preparing lunch. Try to do some preparation tasks on a weekly basis to free up time in your daily schedule.

7. Evaluate the remaining time that is available. Block out spaces of time to work on your to-do list items that were generated from your goal planning.

8. Follow the schedule, and be sure to keep appointments with yourself and your goals. It will take some practice and revision to make the schedule work.

9. Make time to deal with stress. Following a set schedule may initially create some stress, but that is not always a bad thing; it could motivate you to keep moving and get things accomplished. However, don't over commit yourself. If you find the schedule is unreasonable, revise it as necessary. You may have to revise your goals as you go if you find that they can't be achieved in the time you have available.

10. Analyze the tasks as you do them. It's a good idea to think about delegating some of them or working smarter to make tasks take less time.

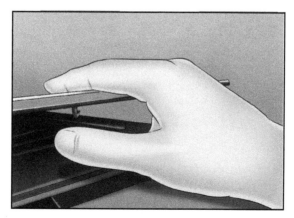

11. Stop every task at the allotted deadline and move on to the next one, unless it is an urgent job. Budget more time to complete the task at a later date. This will keep you from getting distracted and missing appointments.

12. Use clocks and timers to mark the beginning and end of scheduled tasks.

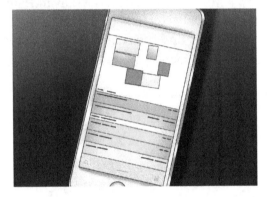

13. Review your schedule on a weekly or monthly basis, and create a schedule for the upcoming month or week.

Workplace Communication Etiquettes

Appropriate business etiquette and manners are essential for building relations and communicating in the workplace. Being civil, showing empathy, a team-building attitude, presentability at work and using proper body language are some of the traits of a successful professional. This chapter describes the communication etiquettes required in a workplace environment, including the professional standards for answering the phone, writing a business email, communicating in a meeting, being professional on social media, etc.

Workplace communication etiquette involves commonly accepted norms and behaviors used while communicating with others in the workplace. Some aspects of workplace etiquette relate to basic standards of appropriateness when communicating with others. Increased reliance on technology for communication has contributed to heightened expectations for workplace etiquette through certain communication tools.

General Purpose

Norms of etiquette are intended to serve as a guideline for behaviors that are generally acceptable and expected in certain environments. By adhering to basic etiquette, you help make those around you comfortable. Workplace etiquette improves your working relationships. Workplace communication includes a number of basic norms about appropriate ways to communicate with superiors, colleagues and subordinates. It also offers some standards for effective communication through certain communication devices.

Common Etiquette Tips

A key point to understand about communication etiquette is that much of the message impact with communication takes place through nonverbal gestures and vocal tone. Certainly, what you say or put in writing has impacts others; however, the website A to Z of Manners & Etiquette points out that the way you dress and your hygiene convey messages open to interpretation by others. Regarding specific things to say -- or not -- simple polite manners like saying "please" and "thank you" go a long way. Avoid sexist, racist or otherwise discriminatory comments about others. Do not interrupt others. Apologize for misstatements or wrongdoings.

Telephone Etiquette

Telephone etiquette includes a basic consideration for the fact that the other person cannot see you. You have to exercise patience and listen before attempting to speak. While you inherently cannot see the other person, your tone of voice and energy transcend the phone line. Colleagues often do spend a lot of time on the phone in organizations with big buildings or campuslike facilities.

People that work together must often show the same commitment to service with internal customers as they do with external customers of the company.

Email Etiquette

Email is another common communication tool used within companies. Unfortunately, colleagues often neglect basic standards of written communication and get too informal in interoffice emails. Do not write emails when you are angry, as you may regret the message the next day. Use appropriate grammar, sentence structure and punctuation. The reader appreciates it. Make concise points, as people at work may have limited time to read emails. Reply to others promptly to show consideration for their initiative on communication.

How to Practice Cell Phone Etiquette

Steps

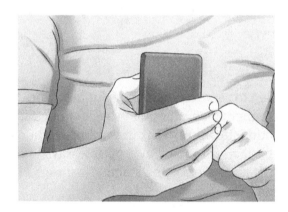

1. The First Principle: It is not other people's responsibility to cope with your mobile phone use; it is your responsibility to use your mobile phone inoffensively. Please note that "inoffensively" is not defined by what you expect others to tolerate, but by what others do in fact find offensive. Ignore this principle, and you are sure to be rude.

2. Following directly from the First Principle: You should assume that someone who asks you to turn your cell phone (or audio player) down or off is in good faith, and you should comply in good

faith. They have a reason for asking, and it's probably not that they're trying to dominate you or hassle you or restrict your God-given right to free expression. (For example, people with temporal lobe epilepsy may find that certain sounds trigger seizures, and some people have neurosensory issues that cause extraneous noise to be a severe difficulty rather than a mild annoyance.).

3. Stay away from others while talking on the phone. If possible, keep a 10-foot (3 meter) distance between you and anyone else whenever you talk on your phone. Most people do not want to hear what you're talking about.

4. Try not to talk on the phone in any enclosed spaces, even if you're more than 10 feet away from anyone. They can still hear you (because it's an enclosed space) and usually, they're forced to just sit there and listen (and maybe be annoyed to some extent).

5. Don't talk too loudly. Generally you don't have to shout in the microphone to be heard on the other end. In fact, doing so often makes it harder for you to be understood. In addition, shouting on the phone disrupts people around you.

6. Don't put your phone on speaker. Just as many people do not want to hear your end of the conversation, they don't want to hear the other person's either.

7. Do not talk about personal details in public. Personal is just that: personal. If callers want to talk about personal details, tell them that you will call them back later, move someplace where you can have a little privacy, or switch to text messaging.

8. Don't multi-task. Avoid making calls while driving, shopping, banking, waiting in line, or doing almost anything that involves interacting with other human beings. In some situations it puts your life and the lives of others in danger, and in other situations it can bother some people.

9. Know where not to use your phone. Some places are inappropriate for cell phone usage, so avoid talking on your cell phone or having it ring while in the following places:

- Bathrooms
- Elevators
- Hospitals
- Waiting rooms
- Restaurants
- Auditoriums
- Taxicabs
- Buses
- Trains
- Meetings
- Libraries
- Museums
- Places of worship
- School
- Lectures
- Live performances
- Funerals
- Weddings
- Movie theaters
- While visiting relatives
- Turn your phone off at any time that you are asked to when on a plane.
  - Or, in fact, anywhere else where people are likely to be disturbed, unless it is important and you can't go anywhere.

10. Don't use your phone when having a meal with someone. Ideally, you should turn it off entirely. If you're anticipating an important call, let the person you're with know beforehand that you're expecting a call that you'll need to take. No matter what, don't hold a conversation at the table; step away, follow step 1, and don't stay away any longer than you would for a bathroom break. Never text at the table, even if the face-to-face conversation dies down. It will be seen as disrespectful.

11. Turn off your phone at the movie theater. Even if your phone is on vibrate, people can hear it during quiet parts of the movie. The light from your phone's screen is also very distracting. Don't check the time, don't check your text messages; just turn it off until the movie is over. If you get an important call that you must answer, exit the theatre before taking it.

12. Learn to text. When you're in an enclosed space, or you can't put yourself 10 feet out of everyone's

way, it's inappropriate to talk but it's potentially acceptable to receive and send text messages. In such cases, keep the following rules of texting etiquette in mind:

- Use the vibrate feature instead of an audible text alert.

- Only text when you're standing still or sitting and out of anyone's way. Don't text while you walk or drive.

- Don't text while doing anything that requires you to be attentive, such as waiting at an intersection for the pedestrian signal.

- Don't text while at a meeting or conference. You should give the speaker your undivided attention.

- Limit phone use during gatherings with your friends. Some friends (with or without cell phones) will find it annoying and inconsiderate.

- Avoid sending others text messages containing anything that you would not say in real life. It is very hard to convey tones and sarcasm in texting and email, so realize that some things may come across as sounding unusual or even offensive. Never send a message with sexual overtones, or one that could be construed as a threat.

How to Answer the Phone at Work

Projecting a professional image at work is important for career success. Answering the telephone is something that almost every employee does, regardless of his or her position in the company. Answering the right way will project a positive tone, help the caller feel comfortable, and set you up to help answer whatever questions he or she may have.

Part 1. Picking Up the Phone

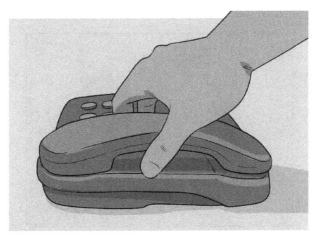

1. Answer quickly. If you are in a business setting, it is rude to keep people waiting. Get to the phone and answer before the third ring.

2. Put the phone up to your face. While you want to move quickly when answering the phone, you should be patient enough to actually get the mouthpiece to your face. Make sure you don't start talking until the phone is right up against you so that the person on the other end doesn't miss any information.

3. Take a deep breath before answering. Once the phone is up to your face, take a deep breath before giving your introduction. This will help you keep calm and controlled, making it easier to speak slowly and collect your thoughts.

4. Introduce your business and yourself. You want to make sure the other person on the line has called the right place and person, so make sure they know who you and your company are. Make sure you lead with the business name. You may want to give yourself a scripted greeting so that

you don't have to think about what to say when the phone rings. This message will change slightly depending on your circumstances.

- If you are a receptionist, it is important that you identify the whole company, as you are the caller's gateway to whatever they need. Something simple like "Hello, this is XYZ Enterprises, Nick speaking. How can I help you?" is good. This lets the caller know who you and your business are, and gives them an opening to continue talking. If you are a personal receptionist, identify the person you are working for ("This is Mr. Miller's office, Nick speaking"), as that is the person your caller is trying to reach.

- If you are part of an office, let the other person know what you do so they know what kinds of questions they can ask. Identifying yourself by saying "Hello, this is Jessica in Accounting" lets the other person know if they have reached the office or person they want, and if they should talk to someone else.

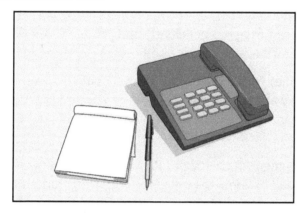

5. Keep a pen and notepad near the phone. This will let you jot down information quickly if the person want to leave a message or give you other information. You don't want to keep your caller waiting while you search for something to write with.

Part 2. Talking on the Phone

1. Smile as you speak. Even if you aren't in a good mood, putting a smile on your face and faking it can help you sound more pleasant to the person on the other end. It will probably help your mood a little bit as well.

2. Speak clearly and professionally. This is a professional setting, and it is important that both you and the other person understand each other clearly and precisely. Speak slowly and enunciate your words to make sure your information gets across.

- Avoid slang words like "Yep," "Sure," or "Nah." Instead speak with clear words like "Yes" and "No." You don't want any confusion between you and the caller over what either person said. Don't forget common polite phrases such as "Thank you" and "You're welcome" when appropriate.

- If you need to give someone specific numbers or letters, say passing along a name or phone number, it can be good to familiarize yourself with the phonetic alphabet. That way you can avoid confusion over letters that sound similar, like "B" and "V," with helpful hints like "V as in Victory."

3. Address the caller professionally. Use the person's title ("Mr. Jones") and not their first name, especially if you do not know the caller personally. Make sure you remember his name, and address him with it during the conversation.

- It may be helpful to write down the person's name after you get it in order to help you remember.

4. Transfer the person if necessary. If someone is calling you at work, he probably has a specific problem or issue he needs resolved. If you don't know how to answer a question or concern, don't try. Instead, offer to transfer him to someone who can help. This also shows that you are interested and willing to help solve your caller's problem.

- Many office phone systems will have a way to transfer calls. Make sure you know if your office does, and how it works. If not, get the right person's number, and pass that information to your caller.

- Be as polite as possible when doing this, and offer the transfer. Say something like "I'm afraid I can't answer that. Would you like me to transfer you to Brian, who can help you?" Make sure the person on the other end agrees before changing the call.

- If someone else isn't available, offer to take a message. Just remember to pass that message along.

5. End the call professionally. A clear and polite "Thank you" or "Good bye" lets the other person know that the conversation has finished and she can hang up. There shouldn't be any confusion over whether or not the conversation should continue.

- Let the other person hang up. She initiated the call, so you want to let her finish whatever she needed when she called in the first place. If you hang up when the caller isn't ready, it can appear rude, or you might miss important information.

How to Answer a Phone Call from Your Boss

Incoming phone calls from your boss can sometimes trigger feelings of anxiety, especially if your boss typically makes you feel nervous and less confident. The best ways to handle phone calls from your boss are to practice professional phone etiquette at all times, and to stay prepared to receive assignments and inquiries related to your job.

Part 1. Practicing Professional Phone Etiquette

1. Answer the phone call within two to three rings. This makes you seem productive and busy. Answering the phone too early can make it seem like you're not too busy, while waiting too long before answering makes it seem as though the caller isn't a priority.

- In a professional setting, you should do this regardless of who's calling you. Don't reserve this or any point of phone etiquette for when your boss shows up on your caller ID, since every co-worker, client, and vendor will be more receptive to a professionally polite demeanor. Plus, you can never know for sure when your boss might be calling from another line.

2. Use a professional greeting. When you answer the phone, strive to be professional and pleasant. For example, if incoming calls are generally from other co-workers in your organization or if you know your boss is on the other end of the line, say, "This is John Smith. How can I help you today?"

- For larger organizations with multiple departments, you might also wish to include your department in your greeting: "This is John Smith in Sales. How can I help you?"

- When answering a phone call from an outside line, you should state the name of your company, even if you suspect your boss might be the one calling. For example, you might say, "Good afternoon. This is ABC Widgets, John Smith speaking. How can I help you?"

3. Swallow food or spit out chewing gum. It's best to do this before you answer the phone, but if you are unable to do so in time, your next option is to complete the action in as quiet and discreet a manner as possible. Talking with food or gum in your mouth can make you sound unprofessional, and can often be detected by the caller on the other end.

4. Speak clearly and directly into your mouthpiece. This prevents miscommunication between you and your boss, which can cause problems down the road. Also, your boss may become frustrated if he or she has problems communicating with you due to muffled talking and poor audio quality.

- You should also try smiling as you answer and talk on the phone. Most callers, including your boss, can hear a smile through your voice and tone. This can reflect favorably on your boss, especially if you work in industries associated with sales and customer service.

5. Give your boss your full attention. When your boss is on the phone, make sure you pay attention. Stop whatever you're working on--even if it's an assignment your boss gave you earlier--and be prepared to listen to what your boss says.

- As a general rule, avoid responding to external distractions when your boss is talking with you. For instance, if a co-worker walks into your office while you're on the phone, politely gesture to the phone in your hand to indicate your current inability to speak.

Part 2. Talking To your Boss

1. Take notes while talking to your boss. This helps you stay prepared in the event your boss gives you important information such as times, dates, addresses, or directions for a specific task. This also allows you to jot down any questions you might have for your boss in return.

- Consider keeping a notepad and pen on your desk or in the top drawer, where it will be readily accessible. Having a notepad nearby will allow you to take notes for both planned and unplanned phone calls.

- If you don't have a notepad available but you're sitting at your computer, you can open a blank note or word processing document and take notes using that. Be aware, however, that your boss will be able to hear any loud typing you do; you'll need to take extra care to demonstrate active listening, so that your boss will be less inclined to wonder if your keyboard clicks are truly related to the conversation.

2. Stay calm. Take a few quiet, deep breaths, and take a sip of water if needed to help you stay calm. Symptoms of anxiety can be heard over the telephone, especially if you're breathing hard, or your voice sounds nervous and shaky. Staying calm also helps you feel and sound more confident and in control.

- If you know your boss is about to call, try taking a short walk beforehand to release nervous energy. Even a walk around your office or department can help. Just make sure you're back with plenty of time to spare for your boss's phone call.

- If you need to calm down immediately before or during the call, try some deep breathing. Inhale as quietly as possible through your nose over a span of four to five seconds; hold for another three seconds, then exhale quietly over another four to five. The increased oxygen should help release tension and clear your mind.

3. Practice active listening at all times. Since your boss isn't speaking to you in person, it's important that you clearly understand everything he or she tells you over the phone. Don't be afraid to ask your boss to repeat and explain things you didn't hear or understand correctly the first time.

- In fact, it might be a good idea to ask for clarification or to confirm details periodically, even if you have a clear understanding of your boss's instructions. This might be as simple as summarizing the instructions in your own words before hanging up. By demonstrating active listening, you assure your boss that you were paying attention and present an overall professional demeanor.

4. Answer briefly and to the point. This conveys preparedness and allows your boss to get to the root of the call with few distractions. In most cases, your boss is busy, and likely just wants information pertaining to the reason he or she called. Unless your boss specifically asks for all the details, try to deliver exactly what your boss wants.

- Again, this doesn't mean you shouldn't ask for clarification as needed. Your boss is likely busy, but it is usually better to spend an extra 60 seconds now asking your question than forcing yourself or your boss to spend hours correcting your mistakes later on. If you have more questions than time allows, consider asking your boss if there's another co-worker or a set of written instructions you can refer to for additional clarification.

5. Do verbal head nods throughout the conversation. Verbal head nods are statements such as "yes," "okay," "I understand," and "I see" -- all of which indicate you're listening actively to your boss.

- Of course, these verbal head nods should be placed appropriately within the conversation. Wait for a pause after an instruction or explanation before making this sort of remark.

6. Maintain a positive attitude throughout the call. Having a positive, can-do attitude shows your boss that you're confident, competent, and not afraid of taking on challenges associated with work. For example, if your boss calls to talk about a problem, discuss possible resolutions you can implement.

- Even if your boss is critiquing your work or behavior, be as receptive as possible. Acknowledge the criticism by summarizing it in your own words, then discuss possible solutions to that point of critique. You can voice any honest concerns you have about going forward, but you should avoid making excuses for past mistakes or issues.

- When you have to raise concerns or explain past problems, make "I" statements instead of "you" statements. This prevents your boss from going on the defense, and responding with angry or negative statements. For example, if your boss calls to speak with you about a project you didn't finish on time, say "I ran into problems gathering resources" instead of "You didn't give me all the resources on time."

7. Thank your boss for taking time to call you. Although your boss called you, and not the other way around, thanking your boss for calling you is a great way to express appreciation for his or her time. For example, say "I know you're having a busy day; thanks for taking time to call me."

- This is true in nearly any phone call with your boss, but it is especially important if your boss was calling to explain a project, express a concern, or critique your work. The goal is to demonstrate your eagerness to do a good job on the tasks given to you, and thanking your boss for his or her time acknowledges that your boss's call will make doing a good job more feasible.

Part 3. Responding to an After-Hours Phone Call

1. Answer the call when possible. If your boss calls you after hours, you should answer the phone as long as doing so does not interfere with non-work priorities. This is especially true if you started this job within the past six months.

- Willingness to communicate with your boss after normal work hours will demonstrate your dedication to the company and to your position.

- If you are unable to answer the phone, however, you should respond to your boss as soon as you're able to. Ideally, this means listening to any voicemail left and calling your boss back within a few minutes. Depending on company culture and the nature of the call, you might be able to get away with a quick text or emailing explaining the delay if a phone call is impossible.

2. Examine your company culture. In some companies, your employer may expect you to remain within contact via phone and email regardless of the time of day or the day of the week. While this may seem unfair, you'll need to accept it as part of your company's culture if you wish to keep working there.

- If you aren't sure what the protocol is, consult with your co-workers. You may learn that it's perfectly acceptable to delay response for a few hours, or you may discover that everyone else answers immediately. Find out what the expected response is and follow through.

3. Stay positive and take action according to the situation. You should always be polite and positive when listening to your boss, even during an after hours call. That being said, you'll need to take a look at each situation individually before determining the right response to it.

- If your boss is offering a general critique or set of instructions, for instance, take notes during the conversation, but feel free to resume your previous non-work activities after the call ends. You can usually save the action for your normal work hours if the matter isn't urgent.

- On the other hand, if your boss calls you about an emergency, you'll need to handle the emergency immediately and according to your boss's wishes.

4. Evaluate your overall job satisfaction. Your boss can't reasonably expect you to be available 24/7 -- however, there's no guarantee that your boss will have reasonable expectations. If your boss routinely calls you after hours and this causes you significant unhappiness or anxiety, it might be time to think about looking for another job.

- You can try turning off your cell phone when you know your boss is making an after hours call, but unless your workplace is unionized, you're probably an "at will" employee who can be terminated at any time. Your boss may back off after getting the message that you won't answer after hours, but it's also possible your boss will respond by firing you.

How to Be Courteous with your Cell Phone at Work

Many employers allow employees to have their cell phones with them when working, but it's important to follow certain guidelines of professionalism and courtesy when enjoying this privilege. Know how to be courteous with your cell phone at work to respect your coworkers and prevent your employer from banning cell phones.

Steps

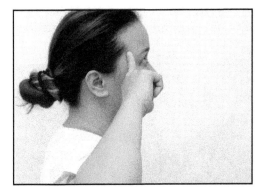

1. Know the company policy.

- Review your employee handbook to familiarize yourself with the guidelines for using your cell phone courteously at work. Some companies have policies allowing employees to use their cell phones on breaks or when there are no clients on the sales floor. Make sure you know the appropriate times to use your cell phone.

2. Turn your ringer off.

- Be courteous with your cell phone at work by turning off your ringer when you're working. A ring tone, no matter how quiet or unobtrusive you might think it is, could disrupt the attention and work flow of those around you. Keep it muted or on a mode that allows it to vibrate and get your attention without distracting fellow employees.

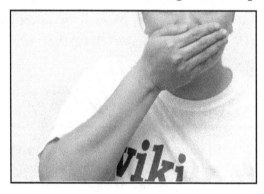

3. Be quiet.

- Use your cell phone courteously at work by keeping private conversations quiet and respectful of other employees and coworkers. Keep your voice quiet and avoid profane language that could offend others around you. If your conversation includes this kind of language, take it outside.

4. Acknowledge other employees.

- Respect other employees if they request that you turn your phone off or take your conversation outside the workplace.

5. Avoid using cell phones in front of clients.

- Clients could view this as discourteous and feel that you aren't giving them the attention they deserve. This could result in larger repercussions with your supervisors, so refrain from using your cell phone when there are clients or customers present.

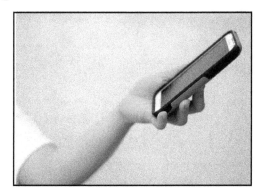

6. Keep it workplace appropriate.

- Remember that you're still at work and keep any conversations or content on your cell phone workplace appropriate. Looking at inappropriate or offensive emails, pictures or videos could violate other workplace policies and get you in trouble, so keep any transmissions on your cell phone professional while you're working.

7. Remember that your phone comes second.

- Your cell phone is second in importance to your job. Keep this in mind when you're working and using your cell phone. Never answer your cell phone in the middle of a meeting, when discussing an issue with another employee or when dealing with a client or customer. Do your job first and answer your cell phone when it's appropriate.

How to Answer the Phone Politely

It's important to have polite, friendly phone etiquette when answering the phone, especially if you're speaking to a stranger or talking in a workplace. When answering the phone, it's important to know how to answer properly so you don't start the conversation off on a bad foot. Answer the phone politely by speaking clearly, focusing on the call, and maintaining professionalism if you're in a workplace environment.

Method 1. Handling Professional Calls

1. Pick up after 2 or 3 rings. When you're answering calls at work, let the phone ring 2 or 3 times before your answer it. If you let it ring more than 3 times, the caller may become impatient and feel that their call is being ignored.

- On the other hand, if you pick up after the first ring, the caller may be taken aback by the quick answer. They may not have had enough time to compose their thoughts.

2. Prepare a professional greeting. When you're answering the phone at your office, you won't always know who is on the other end of the phone. It could be your boss, a customer, one of your colleagues, or even a wrong number.

- A professional greeting like "Good morning" or "How may I help you?" helps get the conversation off on the right foot.

- Even if you have caller ID and think it's a work friend calling, someone could have borrowed their phone. Answering the phone with "Yeah, what?" might give callers the wrong impression of you.

3. Identify yourself and your organization. In business situations, it's most appropriate to answer the phone with your name and company. For example, say "Thank you for calling Smith's Auto Body. This is Joan, how may I help you?"

- Many offices have their own scripting for answering the phone, so make sure you follow the rule your company has set out. If you're not sure of your company's phone scripting, ask your supervisor.

4. Nicely ask who's calling if you don't know. Often, the person will not only give you their name, but also provide information about why they're calling. If you don't have Caller ID, didn't recognize the number, or didn't hear what the person on the other line said, prompt them again by saying "May I ask who's calling?"

- Once the caller has introduced themselves, address the caller properly by the title they provide. If they say their first and last name, and you want to be more professional, call them by their last name.

5. Speak directly into the mouthpiece. Rest the phone gently against your cheek and speak into the mouthpiece that should naturally fall near your mouth. Don't worry about putting the mouthpiece too close to your mouth or having to speak loudly.

- If the person you're speaking to asks you to raise your voice, you can speak a little louder. Otherwise, keep your voice at a normal conversational level.

6. Avoid using slang or profane language. When you're answering the phone at work, you represent your company to whoever you're speaking with on the phone. Speak politely and avoid using slang, cursing, or bad language. Even if the conversation becomes heated and the person you're speaking with swears, maintain your composure and be polite.

- Of course, when you're speaking on your personal phone to friends, you can be informal with them and speak how you would in a face-to-face conversation.

Method 2. Answering Personal Calls at Home

1. Answer in a quiet environment. If you're in a loud environment, move somewhere quieter before

answering the phone, or turn down the music or television before answering. You want to be in a place that's quiet enough so that you can hear the person talking to you, and they can hear your responses.

- A quiet environment will also allow you to focus on the caller.

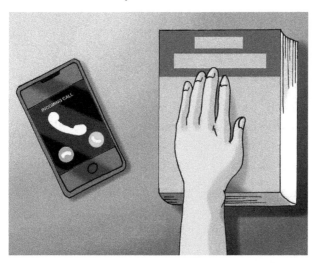

2. Stop your other tasks before answering the phone. Take a brief moment to collect your thoughts before answering. Don't be distracted, as this could lead to miscommunication between you and the person you're speaking to. If you're free from distractions, the person you're speaking to will feel that they have your full attention.

- For example, if you were typing on your computer or reading a book when the phone rang, stop these tasks and concentrate on the call.

3. Say "Hello" and state your name in a pleasant tone of voice. If you don't recognize the Caller ID or know who is calling, you can add "This is Sam." For a more formal answer, you can say, for example "This is the Smiths' residence."

- If you saw on Caller ID that a friend or family member is calling, feel free to say "Hi Tom. How are you today?"

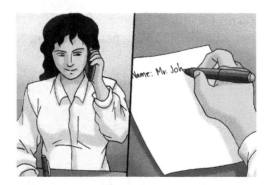

4. Take down the caller's info if the family member they're trying to reach is unavailable. If the caller is trying to reach someone who is not home or is unavailable, say "I'm sorry, Mrs. Simpson, my father is not available right now. May I take a message?" Be sure to record the person's name, phone number, and reason for calling on a notepad in clear, legible handwriting.

- If you don't have a notepad nearby, ask the person on the other line to wait while you quickly go get one.

Method 3. Answering Calls on Your Cell Phone

1. Greet the caller in a friendly tone. When answering a cell phone, Caller ID will typically indicate who is calling you. Say something like, "Hi Steve, how are you?" Even if the number is private or concealed, it's important to answer the caller in a friendly way. Say, "Hello, may I ask who's calling?"

- Since cell-phone calls tend to be more informal than calls to a business or land line, you don't need to say your name when answering the call.

2. Ask why the person is calling. If you don't know the person, be polite by saying "How can I help

you today?" or "What can I do for you?" If you do know the person, you can say something like "What's up?"

- Even if you know the caller, avoid answering rudely. Don't say, "What?" or "What do you want this time?"

3. Speak clearly using your normal tone of voice. Don't worry about shouting into the mouthpiece or over-enunciating your words. Instead, speak slowly and distinctly. If you're shouting or speaking unnaturally, the person you're speaking to may think you're angry or sick.

- If the person on the other end of the line sounds faint, turn up the volume on the side of your cell phone. If they're still faint, ask them to put the mouthpiece closer to their face.

4. Don't answer the phone while chewing gum or food. If you're chewing gum or food, take the time before answering to spit it out or swallow it. You want your mouth to be clear and ready for conversation when you answer the phone.

- Even if you're talking to a friend, they may have a hard time understanding you if you have a mouth full of food.

5. Don't talk to people outside of the call until the call is over. For the duration of the phone call, ignore all outside distractions and give the person on the other side of the line your undivided attention. Don't talk to or joke with other people, and avoid trying to communicate silently while also talking on the phone.

- Even if the person you're on the phone with can't hear the words you're saying to someone in person, they'll be able to tell that you're not focusing fully on the phone conversation.

How to Be Polite on the Phone

Part 1. Using Basic Telephone Etiquette

1. Greet the other caller politely. Whether you are placing a call or receiving a call, be sure to greet the other person politely. Greet the other caller as you would if you were seeing them in person. If you do not know the person, introduce yourself as you would if you were meeting the person for the first time in person. If you know the person you are calling, be sure to identify yourself before starting the conversation.

- Common, polite greetings for placing a call are, "Hello, my name is... How are you doing today?"

- If you are answering a call, a common greeting would be, "Hi, how are you? Thank you so much for calling."

2. Speak in your normal tone of voice. If you talk too loudly into your phone, it may be uncomfortable for the person on the other line. Similarly, if you talk too quietly, it may be difficult and straining for the person on the other line to hear you. By speaking in your normal tone of voice, you will avoid making the other caller uncomfortable.

- If you are worried that you are talking too loudly or too quietly, say "Excuse me, can you hear me okay?"

3. Speak directly into the phone's mouthpiece. If you are talking at a normal volume, the caller on the other line will have difficulty hearing you if you do not talk directly into your telephone's mouthpiece. This is the intended use of the telephone, and using the device properly will ensure that the person on the other line can hear you properly.

- If there is a problem with your mouthpiece, consider purchasing a hands-free headset to eliminate the problem.

4. Do not eat while talking on the phone. One of the most impolite things you can do while speaking on the phone is eating, drinking, or chewing gum. Telephone receivers amplify chewing sounds, and it is impolite to make the other caller listen to these sounds. If you have lunch planned and are on the phone, either wait for the telephone conversation to finish, or ask the other caller if you may call them back after you eat.

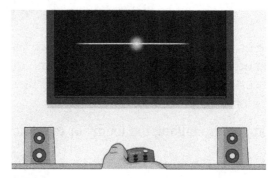

5. Eliminate distractions while talking on the phone. While talking on the phone it is important to limit distractions as much as possible. If you are at home, turn down any music that may be playing and turn off your television. Anticipate what other things may distract you before placing a call and do your best to avoid these distractions.

- If there are other people in the room, consider stepping outside or walking into a different room so you are not tempted to speak with them while on the phone.

6. Ask to call the person back if you have bad service. If you are talking on a cell phone in an area with poor cellular service, it is best to ask the person if you can call them back. Having to struggle

through bad reception can be impolite to the other person, especially if you have to stay in the bad service for some time. Politely ask if you can call the person back at a later date, and apologize for the inconvenience.

- A polite way of asking to call someone back would be to say, "Excuse me, I apologize. I seem to have poor cellular service. May I call you back as soon as possible?"

7. Say thank you and goodbye at the end of a call. It is polite to say thank you at the end of a phone conversation, but it is important to say goodbye as well. Because there are no facial cues while speaking over the phone, it can often be difficult to know when the conversation has ended. By saying, "Thank you for calling, goodbye." it will be clear to both of you that the phone conversation has ended.

Part 2. Talking on the Phone for Business

1. Answer the phone within 2 to 3 rings if you are receiving a call. If you are answering the phone for a business call, it is best to not make the other person wait. Being prepared for a scheduled call will allow you to answer the phone in an appropriate amount of time, while also allowing you time to dispose off any distractions that might take away your attention.

- If the call is not scheduled, it is less important to answer the call within 2 to 3 rings, but you should still answer the telephone as fast as possible.

2. Greet the caller by their professional title. Address the caller by their professional title, like Mr. Brown or Mrs. Smith, instead of calling them by their first names. This is polite business etiquette in person and should be taken seriously over the telephone, as well.

- If you are on a first name basis with the caller, it is okay to drop the more formal title over the telephone.

3. Identify yourself properly if you are making the call. When you call someone and they answer the phone, it is important that you identify yourself and let the person know what you are calling about. This will eliminate any confusion on their end and ensure that the conversation is as efficient as possible.

4. Use professional language. Avoid using slang or profanity when representing your or someone

else's business over the phone. Act as you would at work, with professional, appropriate language. If you question whether something you want to say is appropriate, imagine saying it at work and anticipate whether it would be received well.

- A good rule of thumb is to act on the safe side and ignore saying anything if you question whether or not is appropriate.

5. Ask to put the person on hold if you have to. Whether you are working from the office or at home, distractions will inevitably come up during a business call. If your attention needs to be elsewhere for a moment, it is proper etiquette to apologize and ask the person on the other line if it is okay that you place them on hold.

- Be sure to use the "hold" function on your telephone, for it will mute your side of the line. If you forget to do this, the person on the other end may be able to hear you still.

6. Be patient and as helpful as possible. There are times when business calls can become slightly tense, and staying patient is important for proper telephone etiquette. If the caller is upset about a specific problem, listen to them carefully and decide the best way to help fit their needs. Avoid being rude or impolite in any way.

- If you find yourself getting aggravated, ask to put the caller on hold for a moment. Take this time to calm down, taking deep breathes and regaining control of the situation.

7. Leave concise voicemail messages. If the person you are contacting does not answer, be sure to identify yourself clearly, leave your phone number, and give a brief description of why you are calling. Long-winded messages are impolite and inefficient, as the person on the other line may stop listening after some time. Use proper telephone etiquette while leaving the message and be as concise as possible.

- It is good practice to write down your voicemail message before making the call so that you are prepared if the recipient does not answer the phone.

8. Ask for the necessary information if taking a message. If you are taking a message for someone else, it is important to politely ask for the other person's name, phone number, and reason for calling. Asking for these three things will keep the conversation moving and will have the other person moving on as efficiently as possible.

- After you receive the necessary call back information, thank the person for calling and tell them you will pass the information on as soon as possible.

How to Greet People on the Phone

Polite greetings when picking up the phone make the whole call go much easier, even if you're only responsible for handing the phone over to someone else. Make it easier on yourself and everyone calling by knowing how to greet someone on the phone–be it land line or cell––effectively.

Steps

1. If you've been answering the phone in a slapdash manner, think about how you impact others hearing you. For starters, you don't know who might be on the other end of the phone––it could be a future boss or lover and your first impression has left the caller feeling less than enthused about your phone manner. Remember that a good beginning ensures a good ending. If you find the phone intimidating at the best of times, improving your answering technique will help to boost your confidence because you only have to switch into a polite mode and follow the routine to overcome those initial nerves. Once you've practiced this enough times, it'll feel like second nature and you'll perform it flawlessly.

2. Be aware of the tone of your voice. Without being able to see you, people will draw conclusions about your trustworthiness, reliability and confidence from how you sound. If you're answering the phone for the sake of making business deals, this may be the only chance you get to impress a potential client or business partner. The tone of your voice is impacted by such things as clear or muffled speaking, the mood you're in and the enthusiasm you have for taking the call. You might think that your voice is loud or clear enough to be heard by others, but this is not necessarily so. On the other hand, shouting is just as bad as mumbling and will give the caller a shock. Try to practice your tone of voice with a friend who knows what you're trying to do. Let your friend provide constructive feedback on how you might improve your phone voice.

- Aim for a clear voice that is loud enough to be heard but doesn't shout.

- Lean back and arch your neck up. It is easier to exude enthusiasm in this position.

- Keep your tone of voice pleasant and welcoming. Even if there are other things going on in the background of your life, be reluctant to infect your tone with this unless it's your mom or similar who will listen to your woes. Most other people will only be inclined to listen to a pleasant tone.

- Try to stay standing up when answering the phone. This enables better breathing because your diaphragm is not squished by sitting. In standing up, you'll have more energy and this will come across to the caller in your voice.

- Smile when you answer the phone. The smile will be heard in your voice and keeps a positive energy going.

3. Stop drinking or chewing food or gum before taking a call. Each of these sounds comes through to the caller on the other end of the line and they sound terrible. Other bodily noises to avoid when answering or speaking on the phone include flatulence, burping, smacking your gums together, yawning, mumbling or making popping noises with your mouth. If you have no choice but to sneeze or cough, excuse yourself and quickly cover the phone's sound piece.

4. Answer promptly. A phone that continues ringing leaves time for people to wonder why you're so slow at answering it. When you eventually get around to picking it up, it's possible that they'll be unfavorably disposed to you because they've become a little impatient and they'll wonder if you take them seriously. This is especially important in a work or business context but it can also matter on the home front unless your only callers are family who are already used to slow response times (it won't make them any less frustrated though).

"Hello, my name is Tess from the Legal Services Department. How may I help you?"

5. Greet the caller with a "Hello". If you need to be more professional, say something like "Good morning" or "Good afternoon". Avoid saying "hi" in anything but the most informal context, unless you're keen to sound like a kid. Give your name and if you're at work, give your work title and/or the department you're in.

- A formal example, "Hello, my name is Elizabeth Jones from the Legal Services Department. How may I help you?"

- A less formal example, "Hello, this is Jeremy speaking, from the Brown residence". You don't have to state your family name if you don't wish to. However, if you're in a shared household, you might find this is helpful to a caller looking for one member among several unrelated household members.

- You can simply say, "This is XYZ. May I know who's there on line?" Or, simply giving out your phone number if it's your residence is acceptable, provided you say it slowly and clearly, to allow the caller time to register what you're saying.

- If you're taking calls professionally, always say "Good morning/afternoon", etc, first, before you go onto the company name. For example: "Good morning, this is Mark. You have reached "The Local Deli", how can I help you?" People invariably miss a small portion of what you say first, so if you say the business name as a greeting, such as "local deli..hi.", the caller may well be unsure they have the right number, and have to ask, which makes your business seem unprofessional and can irk the client.

- If the caller is someone you haven't heard from for a while, feel free to express your joy at hearing from them after such a long time. However, don't make them feel as if they have somehow been remiss for not calling you.

6. Listen politely and carefully to the caller's request. During this brief moment, you'll become

aware of whether the caller wishes to speak with you, whether you can continue formally or informally or whether you need to take a message or pass the phone to someone else. During this fact-establishing moment, remain courteous and don't interrupt. If the other person hasn't given their name or it isn't clear to you, be sure to ask for clarification at this early point. Something along the lines of "I'm sorry but I didn't catch your full name Madam" should work.

- If you're so busy that the phone call will be an interruption, then you really shouldn't answer the phone. By answering the phone, you are intimating availability to talk on it, even if only for a few minutes. Never tell someone that you're too busy to talk to them right now; let the answering machine or voicemail do the talking if this is really the case, especially if you're on the line to someone else. To juggle more than one call at once is distracting and potentially confusing for the caller. And to let the annoyance of the interruption come through in your voice is impolite and makes the caller feel awkward.

- Never answer a phone as a means for imprinting your self-importance on the caller. Answering with a brutal "I'm in a very important meeting, I can't take your call right now" is plain rude and is a call that you should not have responded to.

7. If you need to put the caller on hold, then tell them so politely. Indeed, only put someone on hold if you really have no choice. Some people will launch into telling you their problem before you have a chance to intervene, in which case stay polite and let them know that you've heard their request but that you'll need to put them through to the person whose role it is to deal with their matter. If you have to ask them to wait, say something like: "May I put you on hold for a moment, or should I call you back?" rather than asking them in slang to "hang on two ticks and I'll get back to ya".

"Call me back when you get this, thanks!"

8. Leave a comprehensible and clear answering machine or voicemail message. Your answering machine or voicemail is a form of greeting as much as is picking up the phone and answering it directly. Be very careful as to the message that is left on the answering machine. Avoid leaving

anything garbled, mumbled or disorienting, such as a silly joke that only your best friends get. Leave a message that is succinct, clear, friendly and makes an invitation for the caller to leave you a message, with a promise that you'll get back to them as soon as possible.

- Cute, funny, noisy messages on voicemail or the answering machine can fall really flat because only you or your nearest and dearest think they're cute and funny. For the potential client, employer, character referee, etc., such messages suggest immaturity and a lack of seriousness.

Continuing and Finishing the Call

Although these are not part of the greetings aspect of the call, carrying the pleasantness of your greeting through the remainder of the call is important for a successful connection and outcome to each and every call.

"Is there anything else I can do for you Jane?"

1. After the caller has established what they want, use their name to show that you've listened and to establish rapport and repeat back anything that you think needs clarification. Proceed with your discussion, and continue to insert their name frequently as a way of keeping the human connection in place. Continue to listen carefully and make notes if needed. Ask questions about anything that's not clear to you.

"It has been a pleasure talking to you Jane"

2. Finish your call on a pleasant note, even if the conversation wasn't pleasant for any reason. Say something along the lines of "It has been a pleasure talking to you Jane". Listen for a response and don't be too quick to hang up on them.

How to use Proper Business Email Etiquette

Method 1. Crafting the Email

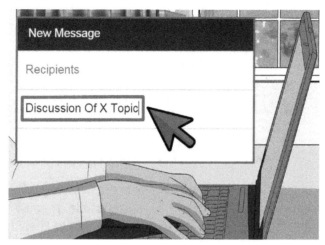

1. Label your emails with a professional subject line. The subject line of your email should be clear and to the point. The subject line should let the recipient know the purpose of the email. Instead of saying "Need to talk," try saying "discussion of X topic.

- The subject should be between six and eight words.

- If the email is being sent for a job application, include your name and the position you are applying for. If you were sending an email to a coworker, you would include the name of the project that the email is discussing.

2. Have a professional email address. If you use your personal email address for business purposes, your email address should communicate your name (i.e. mary.smith@ or Michael-Jones@). Email addresses such as hotmama@, cutiepie@, or mustlovedogs@ are not appropriate for business emails. If you work for a company, you should always use your work email address.

3. Use a formal salutation. Your email should always begin with a professional salutation. "Hey" or "What's up" is not appropriate. "Hi" or "Hello" are preferable. If you are including the name of the recipient in your salutation, do not use a shortened version of their name (i.e. use "William" instead of "Will").

- If someone has a gender neutral name, like Chris Smith, and you do not know whether the person is a Mr./Mrs./Etc., it is best to write "Dear Chris Smith."

4. Use professional language. You should use formal English when writing business emails. Avoid slang and colloquialisms in your email. Abbreviations, emoticons, and text message language (e.g. Lol) should not be used.

- Your email should be concise. Not only is the reader a busy person, but he or she may be reading your email on a mobile device. A short, to-the-point email is much easier to read and respond to than a lengthy, confusing one.

- Try not to address more than one topic in an email. Emails are brief forms of communication. If you cannot address the topic in a brief manner, you may need to pick the phone and call the person.

5. Be aware of your tone. In addition to using clear and concise language, you should read the email out loud to make sure that your email comes across as you intended it to. You do not want to sound harsh or abrupt.

- Remember that your email must speak for itself. You are not there to convey the tone and intent for the reader. Emails do not come with body language and facial expressions. Also, humor does not translate well over email.

6. End the email properly. It is important that you end an email just like you would end any other conversation. You should end your email by saying "Thanks," "Thank You," or "Sincerely" followed by your name. Your emails should also include a signature.

- Your signature lets the reader know how to contact you. It should include your name, company, address, phone, your email address, and a website link if you have one.

7. Proofread before you send. You should read your email multiple times before you send it. Do not rely on spellcheck. People will notice grammatical errors and misspelled or missing words.

Proofreading is particularly important when you are introducing yourself for the first time through email. You want to make a good impression and not be judged by your email mistakes.

- When you are proofreading you should ask yourself: "Am I being clear and concise?" "Did I include any unnecessary information?" "Is there anything I can take out?"

- You should also verify that you are sending the email to the correct recipient. It can be very embarrassing to send an email to the wrong person.

Method 2. Corresponding through Email

1. Know when to use Reply and Reply All. When you choose "Reply," you are sending the email back to the original sender. When you hit "Reply All," you are sending the email to all of the original recipients. Use "Reply All" sparingly and only when it is absolutely necessary to share your response with all of the original recipients.

2. Know the difference between Bcc and Cc. You should use "Bcc" when the privacy of the email recipients is important. This may be useful in group emails or large distribution lists. You should use "Cc" when you need to include other people in the conversation and privacy is not an issue. "Cc" is helpful when you just want to keep someone in the loop about what is going on.

- It is very important that you use these two functions properly. "Bcc" should not be used to secretly pass along private information or to trap people. For example, you should not send an email to your coworker about a mistake they made and "Bcc" your supervisor.

3. Recognize when a phone call may be better. It may be quicker to pick up the phone instead of sending countless emails back and forth. It may be helpful to use the three email rule. If an issue has not been resolved within three emails, you should pick up the phone and call the person. There are times when the phone is more efficient than exchanging multiple emails.

- Keep in mind that this rule is not set in stone. You should use your discretion when deciding it is time to pick up the phone.

4. Know when to start a new conversation. If you need to discuss a different topic with the same recipient, you should start a new email. This will make it easier to keep track of conversations and will keep you from looking lazy. For example, if you have been emailing someone about an upcoming meeting, you need to start a new conversation if you wanted to discuss the outcomes of a project that is being worked on.

How to Improve your Email Etiquette

Steps

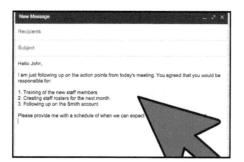

1. Keep your email concise, conversational, and focused. It is harder to read letters on a computer

screen than on a sheet of paper, so keep emails short and to the point. While there is no ideal email length, keep sentences short, about 8-12 words and leave a space between paragraphs.

- In a work email, get straight to the point: "I'm hoping you will..." "I think we should...." etc. right up front, making the case in the following lines. Many people only read the first few lines before deciding to respond or to save for later. Those line should give enough of the "meat" to allow an informed decision. For personal emails, it's often a nice idea to open with a brief personal note before getting into the main point of your email.

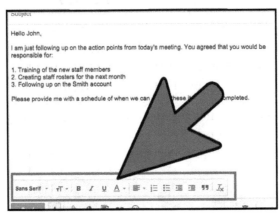

2. Avoid fancy formatting. Changing fonts and colors, inserting bullet lists, or using HTML can make an email look bizarre or render it unreadable for the recipient, even if the formatting looks fine on your computer. Keep it simple.

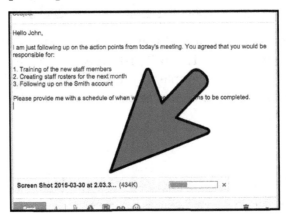

3. Limit attachments. Don't add an attachment unless really necessary. Keep attachments as small as possible. Most email applications can send and receive attachments up to 1 MB, but anything over that can be a hassle for you or the recipient, and even smaller files can take a long time to open if the recipient's email connection is slow. If you need to send a larger file, compress or zip it or use online services that will help you send large files such as YouSendIt.com. If you need to send multiple pages, such as meeting plans or large text corrections, send a fax or a typed set of pages in a letter.

- Don't zip email attachments unless necessary. Unless an attachment is too large to send otherwise, you risk wasting your recipient's time and possibly hinder them from accessing your attachments. Many mobile devices are unable to uncompress zip files. Additionally it's redundant since many common files like .xlsx, .docx, .pptx (MS Excel, Word and Powerpoint) are already in a compressed format.

- Keep in mind that many people or businesses will not open attachments from someone they don't know, and some email accounts are set up to automatically send emails with attachments to the spam folder, so if you're applying for a job, for example, make sure you follow the recipient's instructions regarding attachments. If no instructions are given, send another email to let the recipient know you'll be sending an email with an attachment.

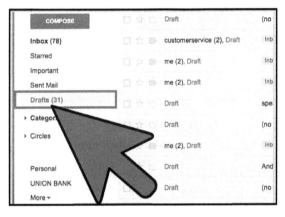

4. Think before you send. Don't send e-mails when you are emotional. Feel free to write the subject and text of the email, then save it. Only add the recipients and send it after you have had time to think about what you are sending; you might change your mind and be better off for it.

- Email has also become a tool to ask or tell people things that you would normally never say face-to-face (ever wonder why you become a different person instinctively online?). If you are sending someone anything, reread it and ask yourself if you would say this to them if they were right next to you, or face-to-face. If it's on a touchy subject, read it twice.

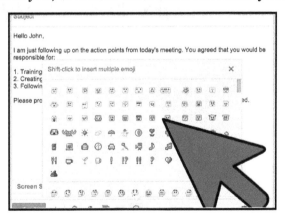

5. Be careful using abbreviations and emoticons. This may be acceptable in an informal e-mail such as with a friend. However, in a formal letter you wouldn't have to tell someone that you're "laughing out loud," people may find it inappropriate, and could feel you are being frivolous.

- Some abbreviations, such as "BTW" for "By the Way," are commonly used in emails and are generally acceptable except in formal, professional emails.

Method 1. Writing New E-mails

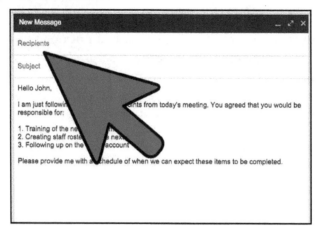

1. Use the recipient fields correctly. Addressees in the "to" field are expected to take action, and those on "CC" are for keeping colleagues or bosses informed.

- Be careful about requesting ACTION from more than one person in the "To:" field. This can lead to multiple efforts for the same task, or no effort because it's assumed someone else is handling the request.

- If sending an e-mail to a list of people whose addresses you want to keep private, put them all in the BCC field and put your own address in the "to" field.

- If you want to phase someone out of the thread (for example, if they have introduced you to someone else, and now you and that person are working out some details and you don't want to bog down the inbox of the introducer) move the person's address from the "to" or CC field over to the BCC field.

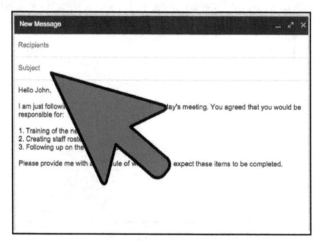

2. Make the subject line useful. A good subject line provides a useful summary of the email's content, preparing the reader quickly. Email inboxes are frequently swamped, so a good subject line helps the recipient determine the priority of your email. It also helps to prevent your email from being deleted before it has even been read. Since the subject is the first thing your recipient sees, keep it error free, concise, and avoid generic lines such as "Hi," "What's up," or the recipient's name (the latter may be blocked by anti-spam filters).

- Avoid prioritizing your messages for the recipient. Get out of the habit of marking every email as "Urgent." or "High Priority" or your emails will end up being treated like the boy who cried wolf and they'll all get ignored. It is irritating and presumptuous to assume your e-mail request is higher in the queue than anybody else's, especially in a work context. Be gracious enough to give the receiver credit for working out for themselves how to prioritize your message.

Method 2. Replying to E-mails

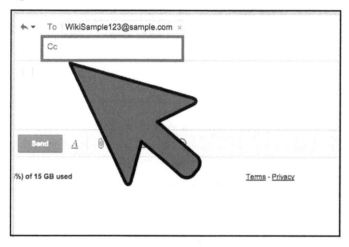

1. Be careful of who you copy on replies. If you reply to a message and then CC: a third-party that the original sender did not include, be certain in your mind that the original sender will not be upset about it. This information may have been "for your eyes only". This is especially important if the original sender is your work supervisor. Be cautious about using BCC:. This can backfire if the person being BCC:'d replies back, not having seen that their copy was a blind one.

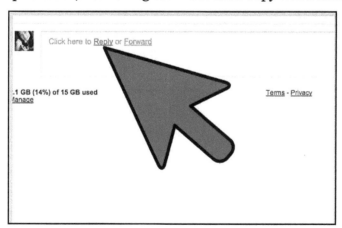

2. Determine to whom you should reply. Emails sent to you solely generally require that you reply only to the sender, but for emails sent to several people, you may need to choose the "Reply to All" option to send your response to everyone. Be judicious; using "Reply All" all the time creates returns in abundance and leaves messages languishing in the in-boxes of many people. Consider the consequences of receiving an email, hitting reply all and it goes out to twenty people and then those twenty people hit reply to all; it can compound very quickly into hundreds of thousands of

emails and everyone feels compelled to hit "reply all" as a means of keeping everyone in the loop because nobody knows who is meant to read it and who is not.

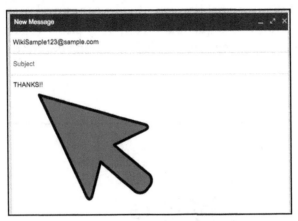

3. Think twice before replying to just say thank you. Some people don't want an email that says "Thanks." This takes additional time to open the email and read it just to read what you already know. Some people include a line that says "NTN" – "No Thanks Needed."

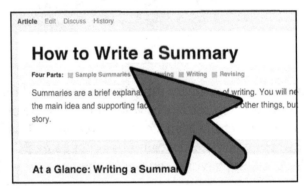

4. Summarize long discussions. Scrolling through pages of replies to understand a discussion is annoying. Instead of continuing to forward a message string, take a minute to summarize it for your reader(s).

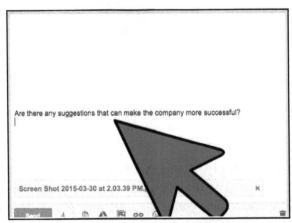

5. Be sure to include info that you are responding to. Many people, and companies, write and respond to hundreds of emails every day. Avoid sending an indistinct email that says only 'Yes'. In-

clude the question that the recipient asked so they know what you are responding to. Avoid making the recipient scroll down more than a single message in the history.

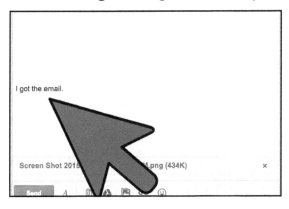

6. Reply promptly. If you need to do some research or some thinking before you respond to an email, or if you're too busy to write a full response promptly, send a short response letting the sender know that you got the email and advising when you will respond.

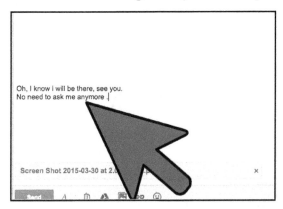

7. Be proactive. When replying to an email, you can save everybody some time by anticipating any questions or concerns your reply may elicit. Address these in your reply before somebody has to send a new email to ask about them.

Method 3. Some Basic Don'ts

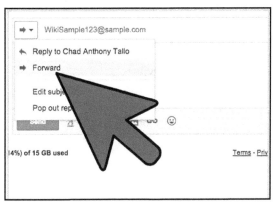

1. Don't forward emails that are private. For example, avoid forwarding an email containing a

secret, especially if the person you're e-mailing doesn't want you to. Doing so can possibly cause the recipient to lose trust in you, and you could possibly have your relationship messed up. You certainly do not want that to happen.

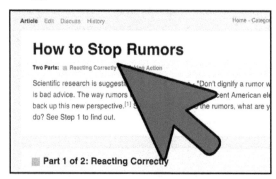

2. Don't spread rumors about people. If you feel tempted to do so, put yourself in the other person's shoes, and think about how you would feel if that person spread rumors about you. For example, if your friend has a reputation for being mean and bossy, think about how you would feel if your friend told your other friends about one of your quirks. You wouldn't be very happy, right?

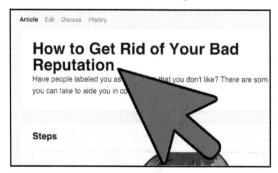

3. Avoid discussing people's private business. For example, avoid letting your friend know that her friend broke up with an ex-boyfriend. Email isn't completely private, so it's possible that the person whose business you're discussing could see the emails and become mad at you and/or embarrassed, and this could mess up your relationship with the person.

4. Avoid flaming. Flames are basically insults sent online to offend you, so it's important not to send flames to other people or start flame wars. This could make the other person mad, and you could also have your account suspended for this.

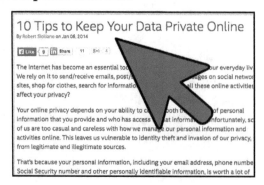

5. Avoid sharing the personal information of others without permission. This can be anything,

from a person's age to the name of the school that he or she goes to. Put yourself in the other person's shoes -- how would you feel if someone gave your friend the address of your house? You would not be very happy, so be sure to obtain permission before sharing someone's personal information with others over email, or don't do so at all.

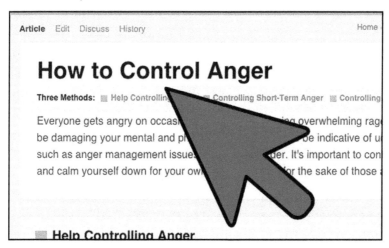

6. Don't send an email when you're angry. It will show you are angry and you can upset the person. For example, if you're angry at someone at work, and you email that person a large rant in all caps, this could cause the person that you emailed to become irritated. This is the same thing with replying to emails; if you're angry at someone for sending you a particular message, hold off replying until you have calmed down.

How to Practice Business Meeting Etiquette

Arrive Early

Arrive to the location of the business meeting at least 15 minutes early. This allows you to find a seat and get situated before the meeting starts.

Follow the Agenda

The chairperson of the meeting should circulate a meeting agenda to each participant at least one week in advance. Participants should call the chairperson to express any concerns about the agenda at least 48 hours prior to the meeting. The chairperson and concerned participant will then have time to determine if changes need to be made. The agenda should also mention the meeting's start and ending times as well.

Be Prepared

Each participant should come to the meeting with all of the materials and data she will need and an understanding of the meeting topic.

Take Breaks

Meetings should have a break every two hours. Breaks should be 20 minutes long, and meal breaks should be 30 minutes long.

Follow the Dress Code

The chairperson should indicate what kind of attire is required for the meeting, either business casual or business formal, and participants should follow that rule. A representative listing of the attire would be helpful as participants may have differing views on what business casual and business formal is. For example, when listing the meeting as business formal, you can indicate that a button-down shirt and khaki pants are sufficient.

Speak in Turn

Keep the meeting organized by only speaking when you have the floor. Ask questions during the designated question period, and raise your hand to be recognized by the chairperson as having the floor. Do not interrupt someone while they are speaking or asking a question.

Listen

You may find that many of the questions you have about a topic are answered by the content of the meeting. Listen attentively to the meeting and take notes.

Keep Calm

Avoid nervous habits such as tapping a pen on the table, making audible noises with your mouth, rustling papers or tapping your feet on the floor.

Be Polite With Your Phone

Turn off your cell phone prior to the start of the meeting. If you are expecting an urgent call, then set your phone to vibrate and excuse yourself from the meeting if the call comes in. Unless laptop computers have been approved for the meeting, turn yours off and lower the screen so that you do not obstruct anyone's view.

Don't Bring Guests

Do not bring unannounced guests to a meeting. If you have someone you would like to bring to a meeting, then contact the chairperson for permission to bring your guest. If permission is not granted, then do not bring him.

How to Practice Virtual Meetings Etiquette

Virtual meetings have become an essential part of how businesses run. They're an easy and cost-effective way to align multiple offices, keep remote employees engaged, work with clients and vendors, and basically get stuff done.

While virtual meetings are likely part of your daily work routine, it's easy to fall victim to some major meeting faux pas. That's right, if you have an online meeting from home, and your webcam displays your unmade bed with your Star Wars sheets, that's a problem.

1. Leave the Keyboard Alone

Whether you're diligently taking notes like the model employee you are or sneakily chatting with your work bestie about where to go for happy hour, the sound of your typing is distracting. It's not only distracting everyone else in the meeting (because your laptop's internal microphone is inches away from your keyboard), it's also preventing you from devoting your full attention to the meeting. So either use a headset or pick up your notebook and pen to take meeting notes.

2. Dress Appropriately

One of the magical things about working remotely is the freedom to wear anything to work. It's the dream. However, when you are in a virtual meeting and sharing your webcam, your coworkers will be less than thrilled to see your lazy clothes and bed head.

So take a minute to throw on a clean shirt and brush your hair. The best part of actually getting ready is that you'll feel more focused to take on the virtual meeting.

3. Be Aware of your Surroundings

Your coworkers won't be able to hear your ideas or take you seriously when there is a pile of dirty clothes in the corner behind you. You also want to avoid looking like you work from a cave because of bad lighting.

Adjust your work set up so that you face a window or are exposed to plenty of light. And make sure your background is professional and work appropriate. This means:

- No beds (unmade or made) in the background
- No messy rooms or open closets where everyone can see your clutter
- No random passers-by or super cute pets that will be distracting
- No NSFW artwork or tchotchkes

You should also remove any noisy distractions. While kids and pets may be adorable and you love them to pieces, your coworkers won't like having to talk over a screaming child or barking dog.

4. Mute your Microphone when you're not Talking

There's nothing more frustrating than hearing that alien echo noise from conflicting microphones. Save everyone from the ear-splitting madness by joining the meeting while on mute.

If you're working in an open-office layout, a noisy cafe, or anywhere that has a lot of background noise, make sure to keep your microphone muted when you're not speaking so it gives other participants the ability to chime in and share their thoughts without distraction.

5. Speak up

First of all, when you enter a small meeting (around two to five people) announce yourself when you join. It's awkward to hear the someone-just-joined ding followed by silence. When you hop on the meeting, introduce yourself and say hi — just make sure not to interrupt someone mid-sentence.

Secondly, don't be afraid to speak loudly during a virtual meeting. Your team will appreciate being able to hear you without having to strain their ears. Keep in mind if your team is in a conference room, that means they are all sitting around a single phone speaker or crowded around a laptop. It doesn't hurt to invest in a good microphone set up to help ensure you are heard during virtual meetings.

6. No food allowed

Make sure to eat a snack before your virtual meeting. No one wants to see you stuff your face with chips while discussing important business matters. It's distracting and you won't be able to focus on the task at hand because you have to worry about dropping crumbs all over your keyboard.

7. Stay seated and Stay Present

It may be tempting to check your inbox or carry on a side conversation during a dull moment in a meeting, but don't do it. You might miss out on key information or an opportunity to give input. If you're using your webcam, use attentive body language — sit up straight, don't make big extraneous movements, and don't let your eyes wander too much.

How to Behave Professionally on Social Media

Steps

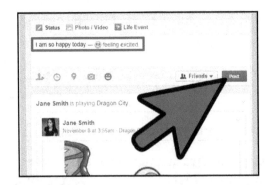

1. Post statements you'd feel comfortable sharing with your boss or clients in person. Before you make any comment or post, consider how you'd feel if your boss or clients read what you've authored.

- Never use foul language or curse words. One of the fastest ways to diminish your credibility is to curse or use derogatory language online. Re-read each comment or post to ensure it is not offensive or contains offensive language. Even innuendos may be enough to cause people to think twice about your character, so take care.

- Avoid sharing emotionally, religiously or politically charged statements. If you wouldn't do this in the workplace, don't do it online either. Don't make statements that could offend or turn off other people. Steer clear of getting on your soap box about political candidates, religions or starting emotionally charged arguments or heated discussions. All of this can lead to disappointment down the career track.

2. Never comment about work online. Whining or complaining about work on social media is akin to announcing that you're not a professional. On the other hand, if you brag about an accomplishment or brashly talk about landing certain clients you'll appear arrogant and there is a risk that your bravado will distress coworkers who think you're stealing all the glory or annoy clients who want things to stay low key. The only cases where talking about work online is acceptable is to perhaps congratulate a colleague or client for an accomplishment, or to express how much you enjoy your work without a specific deal or win being mentioned.

3.Be grammatically unimpeachable. Double check your statements for typos. Before you post, edit your comments. If you want to be taken seriously, make sure everything you write is grammatically correct and void of typos.

4. Post photos of yourself that you consider to be professional. Photos of you showing your abs, cleavage, drunken evenings with friends or making obscene gestures to the camera should not be posted. Ever.

- Carefully select your profile picture. Select from pictures of you participating in a sporting event, at a fun family gathering or a simple portrait would be acceptable. Profile pictures to avoid including wild party pictures or photos of you in a bathing suit or a skimpy outfit (even if you have a banging body). If you must post these, keep them very private and only allow close friends access.

- Be mindful when posting any photo. Any photos posted by you should be clean and "G" rated, no matter where it is in your profile. Delete inappropriate photos or don't post photos displaying sexually charged situations or where alcohol or drugs are involved.

- UN-tag yourself if you've been tagged in unprofessional photos. You may not have control over what your friends post, but you can UN-tag yourself in photos so your network won't be able to view the photo. You can also consider asking friends to delete the photo if it's particularly embarrassing.

5. Share links or other friend's information that may be considered to be universally acceptable. Remain neutral or uncontroversial by not posting links or liking pages that might be considered to be questionable or inappropriate. Be aware that you are as liable as the original poster for liking or

passing on defamatory or other legally dubious statements, photos or content.

- Don't "like" controversial characters or celebrities. Pages such as mainstream news sources or links to globally acceptable activities such as sports, home and garden, autos, children or pets should be fine. However, liking political candidates, religious groups, certain musical groups, controversial movies and television shows may tarnish your reputation with certain people. It all depends on the kind of work circles you move in and how conservative a career trajectory you're following—you'll know whether or not this advice resonates with the choices you've made for your career.

- If you post news and information on your page or on a friend's page, make sure it is not showing bias. Examples of acceptable links include sharing a popular, upbeat news story, sports news or tips on home and gardening. The less controversial and more homely, bland and lacking in politicized/opinionated agendas, the safer you are with sharing it. Again, the extent of sanitization of your information will depend on the career path you've chosen.

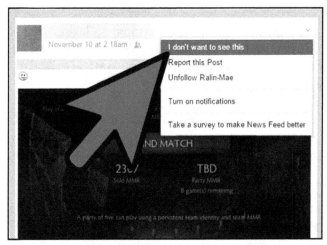

6.Hide friend's comments or information that is deemed to be inappropriate. Remaining professional online means that you don't want to associate with people who post inappropriate comments on your page.

- Steer clear of angry or controversial conversations. If a friend or colleague posts something angry or emotionally charged on your page, delete the comment and call the friend or send him or her a private message. Also, if a friend is fighting with someone on a social media channel never participate or add a comment. This is simply good etiquette, to avoid adding fuel to the flames.

- Private message friends who consistently post inappropriate information or comments on your wall. Ask the friend to stop using certain language or talking about particular topics on your wall.

- Unfriend or hide all posts from friends who cannot abide to your wishes. If a friend begins to take up too much time because you constantly have to monitor his or her behavior on your page, you may need to unfriend this person.

7. Only link, follow or friend people you know and trust. Only associate yourself on social media with people with whom you have a relationship and are aligned with your goal of keeping a professional presence on social media.

- Consider whether you want to friend professional colleagues on social network pages. Although your goal is to maintain a professional personality on social media, you may want to either create a separate page for colleagues and/or clients or make it a policy not to friend people from your professional life.

- Maintain a secure page that only allows friends in your network to view your information and photos. A secure page provides you with more control over what people outside your network can see, allowing you to maintain a better grasp of how you are presented.

How to Practice Instant Messaging Etiquette

Steps

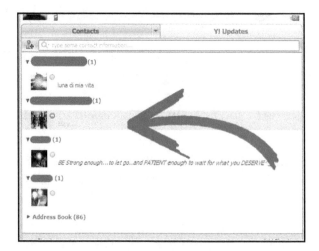

1. Read status messages. Nothing is more annoying than to have your status as "Do Not Disturb," only to be IM'd about a low priority project. Respect a person's status.

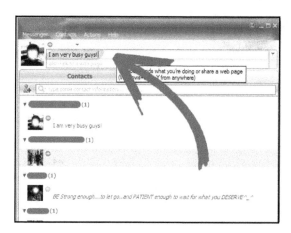

2. Use status messages. If everyone would respect status messages, more people would use them when appropriate. If you're really busy, set your status appropriately.

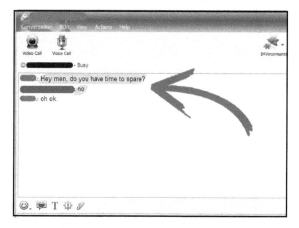

3. Ask if the recipient has time. This gives them the chance to explain that a project is underway, or to ask for 5 minutes to find a stopping point. This is the equivalent of knocking before you enter someone's office.

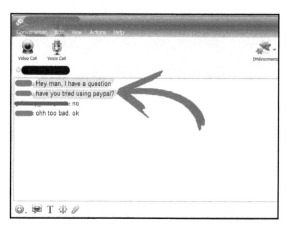

4. Have a purpose. If you're not close friends with the person, don't just send a greeting ("Hey there") and expect them to launch a conversation. You should have a relevant question, or issue to discuss.

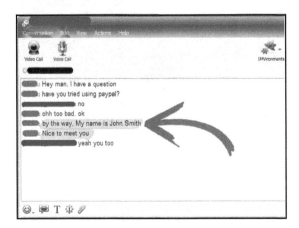

5. Introduce yourself. Many people invite IMs from strangers, and it's perfectly acceptable to send them one. However, be sure to explain (in your first message) who you are; a one-two sentence intro should suffice.

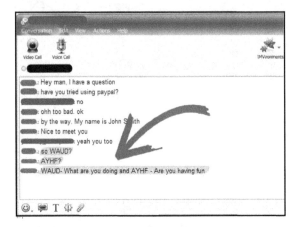

6. Don't abbreviate too much. Unless you know the recipient is on par with your IM savviness, keep abbreviations to a minimum. In fact, for regular IM sessions, it's probably a good idea to avoid abbreviations that you wouldn't use in regular emails or correspondence.

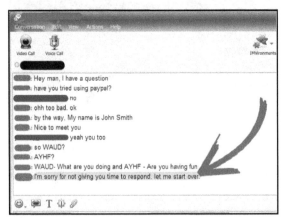

7. Give time to respond. Not everyone types at 200 WPM like you. Conversations get confusing when you type three separate thoughts before the other party can type a response to your first one.

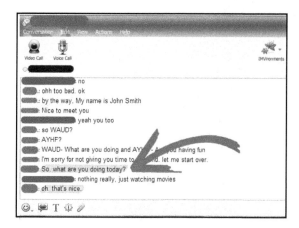

8. Type one thing at a time. This relates to the previous point: be sequential, and one thought at a time.

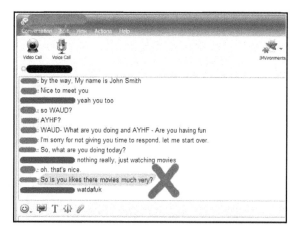

9. Use correct grammar. You're not writing a dissertation, but incorrect grammar frustrates many people, and it confuses communication. Do your best to IM with decent grammar. Use the proper lower and uppercase letters. Do not type in all lowercase letters. Also, do not excessively pluralize words.

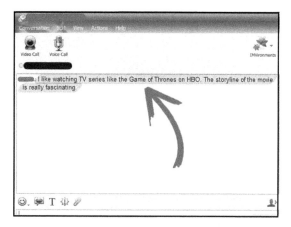

10. Type in sentences. Once again, try to be clear by using complete sentences. It's not a hard-and-fast rule, but a good general guideline to follow.

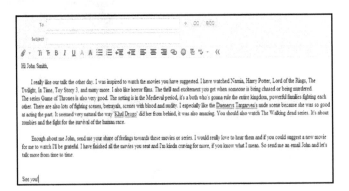

11. Send long text via email. If you want the recipient to read several paragraphs of text, send an email. It's incredibly hard to read a ton in IM, when the screen keeps scrolling because you're not respecting the "one thing at a time" rule.

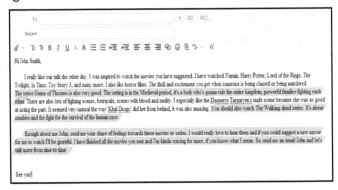

12. Divide thoughts by message. a.k.a.: Don't be too quick with the "Send" button. Make your messages be coherent thoughts, hopefully only one per message. This makes it easier to follow and respond in kind.

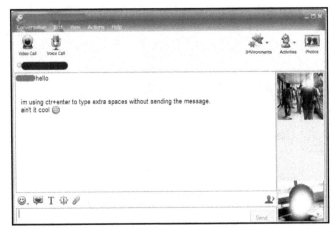

13. Use Ctrl+Enter = a blank line. If you have several quick things that you want in one message together, insert a blank line. In most clients, this is done with Ctrl+Enter.

- Depending on your IM program, this might be Shift+Enter. Experiment to find out.

- If you are using a Mac Client, the hotkey may be Option+Enter. Once again, experiment to find out.

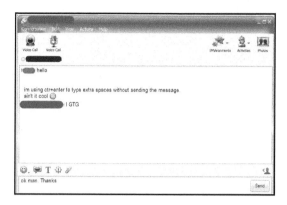

14. Respect brb and gtg. These mean, respectively, "be right back" (brb) and "got to go" (gtg/g2g). These are two abbreviations that IMers should learn and respect. If someone types it, that means something is pulling them away from the message window. Halt your typing (or finish the thought, then type an "OK"), and wait for them to return. If you are the one typing brb be sure it is temporary; don't leave the other person waiting if you are not coming back any time soon. If you know you will be gone for a long time use gtg instead. If you are not coming back respect the other person's time and don't leave them hanging by overusing brb. An ideal replacement may be "Be Back Later".

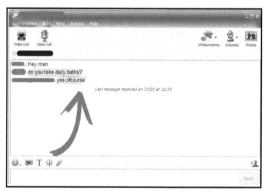

15. Know when the conversation ends. IM sessions aren't clearly ended by hanging up. If the recipient answered your question, and you didn't ask another, she likely considers the session over. If you need something else, ask. Otherwise, don't be offended if you don't receive "Thanks for the IM. Goodbye." Likewise, if you've answered someone's question or you feel the conversation has come to a close, you can ask "Is there anything else you want to go over?" (or similar) and if there isn't, finish off with "It was nice talking to you, thanks for writing. I'll catch you some other time."

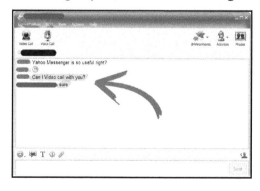

16. Ask if you can call. If your conversation gets intense and typing becomes difficult, a phone call

might help. Ask the recipient if they would prefer speaking over the phone and if calling is all right. It never hurts to ask. Internet voice chat is usually not ideal, but it might be a good idea if you are conversing with somebody you do not know outside of IM.

Hygiene Etiquettes at Workplace

A workplace is a place with constant interactions among people. To ensure professionalism and goodwill, it is vital to practice good workplace hygiene. This chapter discusses in detail some cough and sneeze etiquettes for the workplace, the right use of washroom and the ways to avoid some common hygiene mistakes in the professional space.

Cough and Sneeze Etiquette

Cough and sneeze etiquette refers to simple hygiene practices everybody can take to prevent passing on respiratory infections like cold and flu to other people.

It is especially important that people who are sick with cold or flu practise good cough and sneeze etiquette. However, infections like cold and flu can be transmitted even before symptoms like sore throat and cough let you know you're sick. So even when you're perfectly healthy, it's important to practise proper cough and sneeze etiquette.

Importance of Cough and Sneeze Etiquette

When someone with a cold or flu infection coughs or sneezes, they release respiratory droplets. These droplets contain cold and flu virus particles that can cause infection if they enter another person's respiratory tract (e.g. when they come into contact with their nose).

The droplets released during coughing and sneezing may be inhaled, or they may land on a person's hands or hard surfaces where the virus particles can survive for hours. If a person touches contaminated surfaces, the virus particles may be transferred to their hands. If a person touches their face with contaminated hands, it may cause infection.

How to Sneeze Properly

Part 1. Preventing the Spread of Germs

1. Cover your nose and mouth with a thick tissue: This is the best way to contain your germs. Cold virus, respiratory syncytial virus, and influenza are are passed by droplets in the air. Releasing these viruses through sneezing and coughing is the main way these diseases are spread. Practicing respiratory etiquette (covering your mouth and nose, washing your hands, etc.) can help reduce the chances you'll get anyone else sick.

- Make sure to dispose off your used tissues right away to help prevent them from spreading your germs.

2. Sneeze into your elbow: If you don't have a tissue, the best way to catch your sneeze is to bend your elbow and hold it close to your face while sneezing.

- This works best if you are wearing long sleeves. The goal is to contain the sneeze with your clothing so it doesn't spread into the air.

3. Don't sneeze into your hands: Even though your hands might contain the sneeze, think about how many things you will have to touch with them. You will only be spreading germs around as you touch things.

- While sneezing into your hands is not desirable, it is definitely preferable to not containing your sneeze at all.

- If you have nothing else to sneeze into and sneeze into your hands, make sure you wash your hands immediately. You can also use hand sanitizer for this purpose as well.

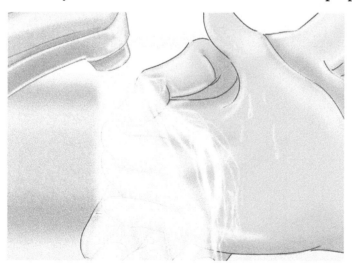

4. Wash your hands: Whenever you sneeze, it is very important to get rid of any residual germs by washing your hands with soap and water right away. This is especially important if you sneezed into your hands or into a tissue.

- In order to ensure that you wash your hands thoroughly, the CDC recommends wetting your hands with clean water, applying and lathering soap all over your hands, scrubbing for 20 seconds, rinsing with clean water, and then drying your hands with a clean towel or letting them air dry.

5. Stay away from people: Sneezes can come on unexpectedly, and no one expects you to keep your distance from other people at all times just in case. If, however, you are sick and are sneezing a lot, do your best to give other people some space.

- This includes staying home from work or school when sick if at all possible. You may worry that this will negatively affect your work or school performance, but staying home when you are sick helps prevent other people from getting sick, too.

Part 2. Sneezing Discreetly

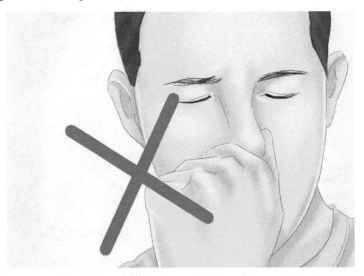

1. Don't hold a sneeze in: Although stopping a sneeze may seem like the most polite thing to do, it's usually not the best option once a sneeze has already started. A sneeze is your body's natural way of expelling irritants from your nasal passage, so by holding your sneeze in, you're holding the irritants in as well.

- In rare instances people have even been injured by holding a sneeze in. Some of the most common injuries include ruptured blood vessels and broken ribs.

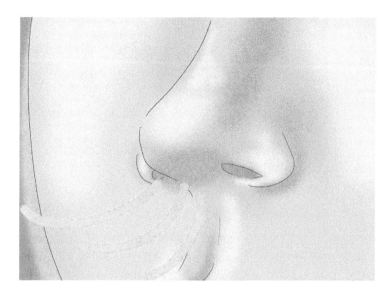

2. Suppress the urge to sneeze: Although you will still be holding on to irritants, suppressing the urge to sneeze is not as bad as trying to stop a sneeze that has already started. There are various things you can try to suppress the urge to sneeze as soon as you feel it:

- Try rubbing your nose

- Try breathing heavily through your nose

- Try rubbing the area between your upper lip and the bottom of your nose

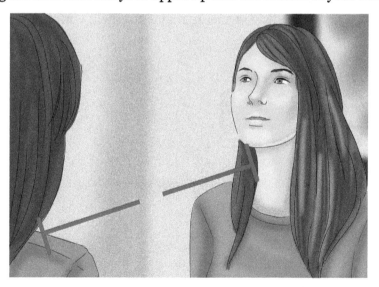

3. Create distance: If you're around a lot of people and you feel a sneeze coming on, the most polite thing to do is to create as much distance between yourself and the other people as possible. If you can, politely excuse yourself and take a few steps away. If you don't have time for that, try turning your body away from everyone else.

- No matter how much distance you create, it's still important to contain your germs by sneezing into a tissue or into your sleeve.

4. Practice your public sneeze: Research has found that most people have at least some control over the way they sneeze and are able to alter their sneezes to be quieter when in public. Try working on quieting your sneeze even when you aren't in public to see just how much control you do have.

- Sneezes do not necessarily need to be noisy. It has been found that that "achoo" sound that many English-speaking people make while sneezing is entirely cultural, not physiological. Deaf people do not make any such noise when sneezing. It might be possible to suppress the reflex to make a sound if you become more conscious of it.

- To practice sneezing more quietly, try clenching your teeth, but still allowing your lips to open, as you sneeze.

- Coughing at the same time as you sneeze might also help you suppress the reflex to make a loud noise.

How to Sneeze Quietly

Method 1. Muffling the Sound

1. Sneeze into something: Keep a tissue or a thick handkerchief with you at all times. A tissue is portable and disposable, but a handkerchief will do a better job of muffling the sound. If you have

no other choice, bury your nose into your shoulder, your arm, or the crook of your elbow. Any fabric or solid body part will help keep your sneeze quiet.

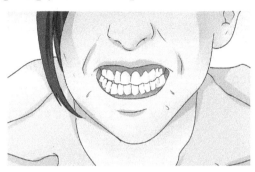

2. Clench your teeth and jaw to suppress the sound: Leave your mouth slightly open so that you don't build up too much pressure in your sinuses. Done correctly, this move should lessen the intensity of your sneeze.

- If you hold your breath at the same time, you might even be able to stop the sneeze from coming.

3. Cough as you sneeze: Make sure to get the timing just right. By mixing up the reflex to sneeze with the reflex to cough, you might lessen the sound and severity of each.

Method 2. Stopping the Sneeze

1. Hold your breath: When you feel a sneeze coming on, inhale powerfully through both nostrils, and hold in your breath until the urge has passed. You may be able to counteract the sneeze reflex.

- Do not plug your nose. Holding your breath can be effective, up to a point, but plugging your nose during a sneeze can have serious health consequences. Among other disturbances of the ear and nasal passages, this can cause larynx fractures, ruptured eardrums, voice changes, bulging eyeballs, and bladder incontinence.

- Bear in mind that while holding a sneeze back might be effective, it also might leave you feeling somewhat stuffed-up.

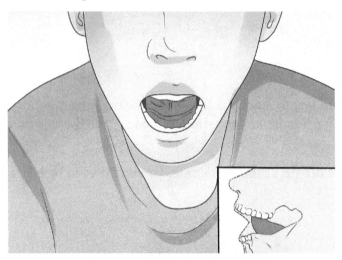

2. Use your tongue: Press the tip of your tongue firmly into the roof of your mouth, right behind your top two front teeth. This should hit the spot where the alveolar ridge or "gum palate" reaches up to the roof of your mouth. Push as hard as you can until the urge to sneeze goes away. Done correctly, this can stop a sneeze in its tracks.

- This strategy is most effective if you do it the moment that you feel a sneeze coming. The longer the sneeze has to build, the harder it will be to stop.

3. Push your nose up: When a sneeze is coming, place your index finger beneath your nose and push up slightly. If you time it right, you might be able to suppress the sneeze. At the very least, this move should lessen the intensity of the sneeze.

How to Practise Good Cough and Sneeze Etiquette

Good cough and sneeze etiquette involves taking steps to minimise the likelihood that someone else will catch your cold or flu when you cough or sneeze. There are many simple measures you can take.

Cover Coughs and Sneezes

1. Cover your mouth and nose every time you cough or sneeze. Use a disposable tissue to cover your mouth or nose if possible.

2. If a cough or sneeze sneaks up on you and no tissue is available, cough or sneeze into your upper sleeve. This prevents your hands becoming contaminated with cold or flu viruses.

Dispose off or Clean Contaminated Products Immediately

1. Dispose off single-use tissues immediately after you cough or sneeze. Try to ensure a waste bin is available so that tissues can be disposed of (e.g. if you're in bed with the flu, put a bin beside your bed so you don't have to get up to throw your contaminated tissues away). If there is no bin, use a plastic bag to store contaminated tissues until a bin is available.

2. If you cough or sneeze onto a hard surface like a desk or telephone, clean it immediately with a disposable disinfectant wipe to remove the cold and flu germs.

Ensure your Hands are Hygienically Cleaned

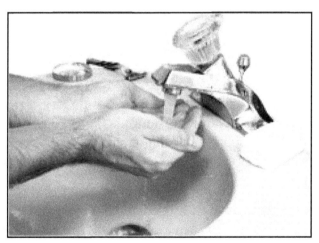

1. Wash your hands with soap and water for at least 15–20 seconds every time you cough or sneeze.

2. Wash your hands every time you touch a contaminated object like a tissue.

3. If soap and water are not available, use alcohol-based hand sanitising products containing ≥ 60% alcohol. These products are also effective in removing cold and flu germs from contaminated hands.

Avoid Touching the Face

1. Avoid touching your face with your hands (especially if you know they're contaminated, for example if you've just wiped your sick child's nose). Touching the face allows cold and flu viruses to enter the mucous membranes of the nose and eyes and cause infection.

Avoid Close Contact with others

1. Stay away from work, school and other busy places as much as possible when you have an illness like cold or flu which causes coughing and sneezing.

2. If you need to go to work or other busy places, avoid close contact with others, for example by not shaking hands and standing at least one metre away.

How to Avoid Common Hygiene Mistakes

Method 1. Cleaning Your Body

1. Brush your teeth: You should brush your teeth multiple times a day. Most dental hygiene experts suggest brushing two times daily, after breakfast and before you go to bed. This will help prevent tooth decay, gum disease, and bad breath. To make sure that your overall oral hygiene is at its best, you should also floss daily.

- You should try to use toothpaste with fluoride because it will help strengthen your teeth and promote a healthy mouth. You can also use mouthwash with fluoride as well.

- When you brush your teeth, you should also clean the rest of your mouth. Ignoring your tongue, the roof of your mouth or the insides of your cheeks can leave harmful bacteria in your mouth that can cause hygiene problems. Run your brush over all the surfaces in your mouth and scrub the surface of your tongue with the bristles every time your brush your teeth.

- Replace your toothbrush every three months. This will ensure that your brush is the most efficient it can be for the best oral hygiene possible.

- See your dentist regularly for check-ups. Most dentists recommend twice a year, but your dentist can recommend a schedule that's best for you.

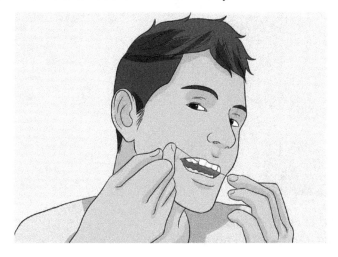

2. Floss daily: Along with brushing your teeth, you should floss every day. This will help combat bad breath and cavities. Each day, you should pull floss between each of your teeth and run it along the edges. Make sure you reach your back teeth as well.

- Don't snap the floss against your gums. This may cause them to bleed, which you don't want.

- If your gums always bleed when you floss, you may have an underlying dental issue. You should see your dentist.

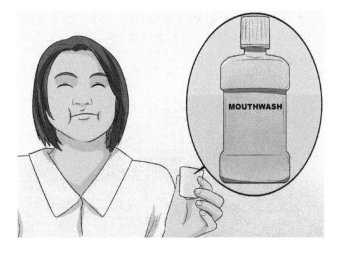

3. Use mouthwash: One way to ensure that you have extra minty breath all day long is to use mouthwash. It helps prevent bacteria and can help fight cavities as well. Swish it around your mouth after each time you brush. You can also use it after meals if you can't brush your teeth to help get rid of odors lingering in your mouth.

- You should never use mouthwash to replace brushing your teeth or prevent underlying causes of bad breath. It is only used to help add a minty smell to your breath and help your other oral hygiene methods.

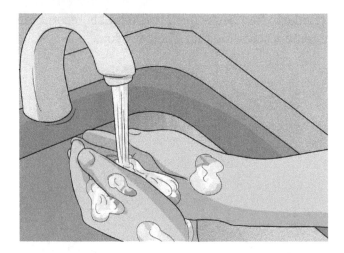

4. Wash your hands: To keep up personal hygiene, you need to make sure that you wash your hands often. Not washing hands often enough is one of the most common hygiene mistakes people make. Common situations where you need to wash your hands are after you go to the restroom after you sneeze, before you prepare food or drinks, before you eat, and after handling objects that are handled by many others. This helps keep you clean as well as stop the spread of germs and bacteria that lead to illness.

- When washing hands, you should lather your soap covered hands in warm water for at least 20 seconds. Make sure to rub in between your fingers and around your nails. This ensures that the soap has time to kill any germs on your hands. You should then rinse the soap off with warm water and dry them with a disposable towel or use an air dryer.

- If you want to further prevent the spread of germs, you should sneeze into your elbow. This helps cover more of your nose and mouth and keep the germs from your hands.

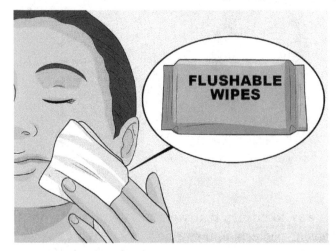

5. Use flushable wipes: Disposable wipes are not just for babies anymore. If you are feeling slightly unfresh, you can use one of these wipes to clean yourself if you cannot get to a shower. They are also good to use if you have to defecate and want to freshen up afterwards.

- You can find these at the grocery or general stores. They are in the adult hygiene aisles.

6. Shower frequently: To keep yourself clean, fresh, and smelling pleasant, you should shower or take a bath daily or every two out of three days. This is the best way to prevent unnecessary body odors as well as prevent the build up of bacteria or germs on your skin. There are some recent studies that suggest that taking a day off from showering every few days is healthy for the skin and helps promote healthy bacteria growth on your skin. Make sure you wash every part of your body, including every part of your feet and behind your ears.

- If you go to the gym, commute on public transit or come into contact with sick people daily, you should shower every day to avoid the spread of germs and to maintain cleanliness.

- Make sure you wash your belly button. It may be an area that you forget about, but numerous odor-causing bacteria can grow there.

- If body odor is a constant concern for you, ask your doctor about an antibacterial body wash.

7. Shampoo your hair: You should wash your hair 2-3 times a week. For most people, it can be harmful to your hair if you wash it every day. If you wash it daily, you can wash out the natural oils in your hair, causing it to break and become damaged. If you have excessively oily hair, however, it may be necessary to wash your hair daily.

- The amount of times a week that your hair should be washed can be different for every person. Be aware of what your hair smells like and pay attention to how oily it gets. Keep a check on your hair to assess how often you should wash it.

- If you work out, do sporting events or take part in any other activity that causes your scalp to sweat profusely, you should wash your hair more often.

8. Cleanse your face: As part of a good overall hygiene routine, you should wash your face every morning and every night. This helps get all the impurities off of your face from the day and any oil that accumulated on your face overnight. It also helps you remove any makeup, moisturizer, or sunscreen that you may have put on your face throughout the day. Washing your face prevents acne and will give you a clean, brighter appearance every day.

- Make sure you pick the right cleanser for you. Not every person's skin is the same, so try a few different kinds until you find the cleanser that works for you. If you need some help, talk to your doctor or pharmacist, who can help you find the right cleanser for your skin.

- You should moisturize after your wash your face. This will help prevent dry, irritated skin and promote skin health.

9. Change your feminine products often: If you are a female and you are on your period, you need to change your feminine products (such as pads or tampons) often. If you do not, this may lead to spills and leaks on yourself and your underwear. If this happens, you should wash yourself or find some kind of wipe to help clean you until you can shower.

- Changing your products frequently will make you feel cleaner and help prevent odors.

- If you find that you smell slightly during your period, you can get feminine deodorizing sprays that are specifically designed for these situations. Apply them according to the instructions on the bottle. Don't apply sprays directly to your genital area, as they can cause irritation.

Method 2. Preventing Odors

1. Wear deodorant: To avoid smelling when your body naturally sweats every day, you should wear deodorant. This will help cover up and block the musty smell of sweat and keep you cleaner. You can also buy antiperspirant, which helps prevent you from sweating and dries up the sweat when you do. Many brands offer a combination antiperspirant/deodorant.

- There are many different types of deodorant and antiperspirant, some targeted to girls and some targeted to boys. You can pick whichever works best for you. Some scents may be too overbearing or not work well with your body chemistry. Just keep trying until you find one that is subtle, keeps your dry, and makes you smell good.

- If you have trouble with excessive sweating, or you continue to have body odor problems despite good hygiene, talk to your doctor. You may have an underlying condition that requires treatment.

2. Avoid overly fragrant scents: You want to smell good, but it is just as bad to smell too much like perfume or cologne. When you pick a fragrance, you should find a scent that is pleasing, but not

overwhelming. If it is stronger than some, you should apply it lightly, putting on just enough for people to smell it but not for it to be overpowering.

- Don't use sprays to cover up body odor smells. They should be used to make you smell nice, but not to try to cover up body smells. If you are experiencing body odor, you should find the cause and take care of it instead of trying to cover it up.

3. Wash and change your clothes: In order to promote good personal hygiene, you should change your clothes daily. You should also wash your clothes often to ensure they are clean and smell fresh. Most clothes can be worn at least two times before you wash them, with the exception of socks and underwear. However, if you think that your clothes have an unpleasant smell, do not wear them without washing them first.

- Any clothes you wear to the gym, while playing sports, or during any other activity where you sweat a great deal should always be washed after one use.

4. Change your sheets weekly: Just like you need to change your clothes often, you need to change your sheets. You sweat at night and loose dead skin cells, and they can build up on your sheets over time. If you change your sheets frequently, you don't run the risk of sleeping in your dead skin every night or transferring the sweat smells from previous nights onto your skin while your sleep.

- You should change your pillowcase more often. Your face has more oils and you may also drool overnight, which also builds up on your pillows as well.

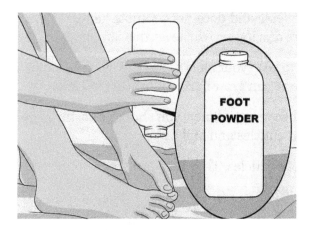

5. Use foot powder: Smelly, sweaty feet can also promote infections like athlete's foot. Using a drying or an anti-fungal foot powder on your feet and in your shoes can help your feet stay drier and germ-free.

6. Watch what you eat: Certain foods and beverages can cause body odor. Avoid foods with strong odors, such as garlic or onions, if you need to smell fresh. If you enjoy these foods, make sure to brush your teeth or rinse with mouthwash after eating if you're going to be in public.

Method 3. Practicing Personal Grooming

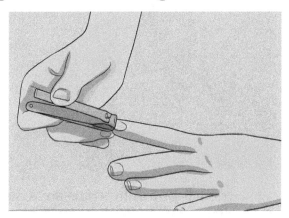

1. Clip your nails: Having poorly groomed nails can cause dirt and germs to get trapped underneath

the nail beds. This is unhygienic and does not promote general cleanliness. You should cut your nails with manicure scissors or clippers whenever they are too long, jagged, or misshapen.

- You should also try to keep your nails as dry and clean as possible. You can spread infection otherwise and bacteria can grow in constantly moist nails.

- To help your nails become healthier, you should moisturize your nails frequently by rubbing lotion into your cuticles and nail beds.

- Don't cut or trim your cuticles. They help protect the nail bed.

2. Brush your hair: To give yourself a put together appearance, you should brush your hair daily. This removes snares and rats from your hair and makes it looks smooth and healthy. It also has the added benefit of spreading natural oils throughout your hair, which promotes hair health. It also cleans and stimulates the scalp.

- Make sure your don't brush your hair too much. This can cause breakage and actually do more harm than good for your hair.

- If you have natural hair, use your fingers or a wide-toothed comb to detangle before going to the brush. This will help avoid breakage.

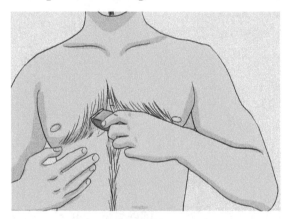

3. Shave certain areas: Having excessive body hair in certain areas can cause body odor or make you look unkempt. Shaving or maintaining your body hair can be an effective hygiene technique because it allows more air to reach the skin, which reduces the amount of odor that is held in the

area. It also has the benefit of highlighting certain areas if your body hair is more sculpted or clean shaven. However, shaving is a personal choice, and you should choose what you're comfortable with.

- Common areas to shave or maintain are the underarms, the chest, the legs, the genital region, and the face. Shaving under the arms and shaving or maintaining hair in the genital region helps reduce odors. These areas are known to sweat profusely and the musty smell can build up in the hair if it is not properly maintained.

- Maintaining or shaving chest, leg, and facial hair is an option, but is not necessary if you don't feel comfortable with it.

- Shave gently with the "grain" (i.e., shave in the same direction the hair is growing). Use shave gel or foam to avoid irritating the skin.

4. Pluck unwanted hair: There are some areas of the body that grow hair that isn't necessarily thick enough to shave. In these cases, you may need to pluck the hair to maintain your personal hygiene. Common areas where these kinds of hairs may arise are on the cheeks, the neck, and the eyebrows. There may also be cases where a dark stray hair may grow on any portion of the body.

- Both men and women have this problem. The areas where the hair grows may be different, but the general need for personal grooming is the same.

- To pluck the unwanted hair, use tweezers to grasp the hair tightly and pull it out. Continue until all the unwanted hair is gone.

How to use Restrooms at Work

For some people, pooping at work is no problem. For others, it can be a source of workplace anxiety. Regardless of which side of the fence you're on, when using the restroom at work there are a few rules to follow. Don't spend more time than necessary in the restroom, and don't point out the habits of your peers. If you have trouble doing your business at work, consider finding a restroom with less traffic so you can relax.

Part 1. Observing Etiquette

1. Be courteous: Don't talk about other people's bathroom habits. If you happen to recognize someone in the restroom, don't mention it.

- Don't make jokes at anyone's expense, and don't draw attention to someone in a stall.

2. Avoid conversation: Don't try to talk to someone in the stall next to you. While you may have a great work relationship with someone, they may not want to have a conversation between the stalls.

- Be considerate of others using the restroom. Don't talk on your cellphone, and don't use the restroom as a chance to catch up with another co-worker. Your conversation could be distracting to someone in a stall.

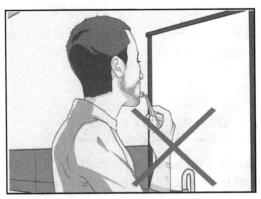

3. Don't linger: Restrooms can have a lot of traffic, especially if you're in a busy office building. Once you're finished, get out. Don't use the restroom for anything other than its intended use.

- Avoid using your workplace restroom to shave or cut your toenails. Other people may be waiting on you to leave so they can relieve themselves.

Part 2. Doing your Business

1. Avoid reading materials: When pooping at work, don't take reading materials into the stall with you. If you're nervous about people knowing what you're up to, then holding a newspaper will almost certainly tip them off.

- Even if you have no problems pooping at work, avoid reading in the stall. You'll take longer, and you may be preventing people who need to use the restroom.

- Don't use your cellphone in the stall.

2. Find a different restroom: If you have trouble using the restroom at work, try to find a restroom on a different floor. Search for a restroom that is not used as frequently and do your business there.

- If your workplace only has one restroom, search for a time when there is not as much traffic so you can have some peace and quiet.

3. Muffle the sounds: If you are worried about people hearing you while you're in the stall, drape some toilet paper across the seat before doing your business. The paper will dampen any noises you might make while relieving yourself.

Part 3. Keeping the Restroom Clean

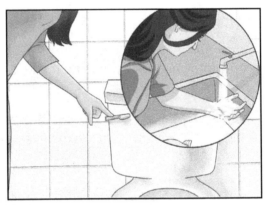

1. Clean up after yourself: Don't make a mess in the stall. Other people have to use the same restroom you do at work, and no one wants to deal with a mess. Be considerate of others and try to be clean in the stall.

- Wash your hands. You should always wash your hands after using the restroom.

2. Ask for air-fresheners in the stall: If you're embarrassed about the smells that come from the stall, ask your supervisor to buy some spray air freshener for each stall.

- If you can't convince your supervisor to invest in any air fresheners, you could bring your own from home, or carry a book of matches. Lighting a match can often help eliminate bad smells.

3. Make sure there is enough toilet paper: If you notice the toilet paper in your stall is running low, refill it. If you don't have access to refilling it, let the person who maintains the restroom know that it needs attention.

4 Eating and Dining Etiquettes

It is imperative to exercise basic table manner while eating and dining. The right ways to chew, eating soup, using fork and knife, using a napkin, stirring a beverage, etc. are important eating and dining etiquettes. This chapter explores these etiquettes with respect to a professional setting.

Eating Etiquette

Nearly everyone eats at work at one time or another, whether its bringing your lunch on a daily basis, stashing snacks in your desk for mid-afternoon and overtime noshing or taking part in a company potluck. While basic table manners and rules of common courtesy apply to eating in the workplace, care must also be taken to respect others' space and olfactory senses.

Follow Company Protocol

Many companies have specific policies about how food breaks are to be taken. Some businesses prefer that employees eat only in a company break room, while others are comfortable with desk snacking and dining if the food is relatively easy to handle. Still other companies want employees to use designated lunch hours and prefer no food at work stations. Consult your employee handbook or talk with human resources to learn more about your company's food policy.

Don't Eat in Front of Customers

Never eat in front of a customer, or eat while talking with a customer on the phone. Sipping a cup of coffee or water during a meeting is fine, but food and client service should never be mixed unless you're at a lunch or dinner meeting. Avoid chewing gum or sucking on candy during customer interaction as well.

Follow Basic Table Manners

When you are eating at work as part of a group, during a potluck or lunch meeting, follow all generally accepted table manners. Keep your elbows off the table, chew with your mouth closed, don't talk with your mouth full and use your napkin liberally. Don't go back for seconds until everyone has had firsts and don't disparage the food.

Clean Up After Yourself

Whether you're snacking at your desk or cooking a messy meal in the office kitchen, always clean up after yourself. This includes busing your table or desk, putting trash in appropriate receptacles, wiping down your table or desk and doing dishes you use from common areas. Don't leave leftover food in the shared refrigerator for too long. Throw away unwanted food before it spoils.

Forego the Smelly Food

Just because garlic sauerkraut is your favorite food doesn't mean that everyone in the office will agree. Leave pungent-smelling food at home and if something you cook gives off a stronger-than-expected odor, air out the room by opening a window or spray the room with air freshener.

Don't Steal.

Never take food that isn't yours from the office kitchen or fridge. Carefully mark your own food with your name so no one will be tempted to steal it. If a plate of cookies or donuts is left on a break room table it generally means the food is available for anyone who wants it, but otherwise, keep your hands to yourself.

Practice Good Hygiene

Wash your hands after eating and brush your teeth if possible. If you've eaten at your work station, wipe down surfaces you may have touched, like your keyboard and telephone.

How to Act during a Business Meal

A business meal can be very important to your success in a company, so it is vital that you know how to act appropriately. Behaving appropriately will help to make a good impression and this is what you want when you are sharing food with coworkers, managers, or even competitors. Make your initial introductions smoothly by familiarizing yourself with the restaurant and using confident body language. Behave professionally throughout the meeting, and gracefully handle things like paying the bill. You should also follow basic etiquette, such as chewing with your mouth closed and keeping your elbows off the table.

Part 1. Making the Most Out of Initial Introductions

1. Research the restaurant ahead of time: You do not want to appear indecisive or nervous during a

business lunch. Doing some research on the restaurant will allow you to know what to expect going into the meeting. You will also be able to choose an entree ahead of time so you can order smoothly.

- You can usually look up the menu online if the restaurant has a website. If it does not, a site like MenuPages may be able to provide this information. Try to pick an entree beforehand, and also a backup choice just in case the restaurant is out of your chosen meal.

- Also, try to get a feel for the atmosphere. You do not want to be thrown off by being surprised by a restaurant's ambiance. Go into the situation knowing what to expect so you can keep your cool during the meeting.

2. Dress appropriately for the type of business function: You will want to get a sense of how you should dress. A business lunch can sometimes be more casual than a formal interview or a regular meeting, but there may still be etiquette regarding attire. Try to feel out what would be appropriate to wear going into the lunch.

- Read over the invitation you would sent again and look for any hints. The sender, for example, may have said something like, "It's a casual restaurant, so feel free to wear something comfortable." In this case, there is no need to wear a business suit. However, do not show up in jeans and a t-shirt. Wear something like dress pants and a nice button-down shirt or blouse.

- If you're unsure what appropriate attire is, it's okay to find a tactful way to ask. For example, you could email the host something like, "I'll be coming from the office, and I usually wear a polo shirt and khakis to work. Will that be appropriate for the restaurant?"

3. Arrive on time or early: You never want to be late for a business meal. It's obvious to everyone who arrived on time when you come in late and attempt to find a seat. By arriving early, you can

observe how seating is being arranged and where you'll be sitting. Arriving about five minutes before your scheduled meal time is socially acceptable.

- Look up how long it takes to get to the restaurant. Make sure you give yourself enough time to find the restaurant and park. If you're taking public transportation, make sure you review bus and train schedules ahead of time.

- It's a good idea to give yourself slightly more time than you think you will need. Something like traffic or a train or bus delay could cause you to take longer than expected. Try to give yourself about 20 minutes of leeway. You can always get coffee nearby or walk around the area if you're early.

- It may be a good idea to swing by the restaurant a day or so before the meeting to make sure you know how to get there.

4. Shake hands and look people in the eye when speaking to them. If you are meeting someone for the first time at this meal, make sure to firmly shake their hand and maintain eye contact while doing so. The same body language that can convey confidence during a job interview should be used in a business lunch. You want to be sure to look confident and greeting someone this way will exude poise and self-assurance. Walk into the meeting feeling secure, standing up straight, and offer a smile, eye contact, and a handshake.

Part 2. Behaving in a Professional Manner Throughout the Meeting

1. Treat your server and the other restaurant staff respectfully throughout the meal: Part of acting

appropriately during a business meal is maintaining comfort during a social situation. This means treating everyone present with respect, including the restaurant staff. Be certain that you say please and thank you, ask questions kindly, and make requests to your server politely.

- You want to make sure you come off as someone easy to get along with. This means you should laugh off mistakes servers made and not respond with anger or hostility if the bill is wrong or your order was screwed up.

- Never send your food or drink back, especially if your boss or superior picked the restaurant. Not only will this make you look difficult, it can come off as insulting or ungrateful.

2. Make wise choices regarding alcohol: Determine what kind of business meal you're attending so you know if alcohol consumption is appropriate. Look around while at the restaurant to see if anyone is drinking. If no one is, don't drink either. If alcohol consumption is acceptable, stick to just two glasses of wine or one mixed drink or martini. Anything more is considered excessive and can also cause you to behave differently. You want to make certain you're maintaining a good image while conducting business.

- If possible, wait until your boss or co-workers order. If your host or your co-workers are ordering drinks, it may be okay for you to have a cocktail.

- However, if your boss is having water or something non-alcoholic like tea, it's a good idea to stay away from alcohol. Drinking when the other party is remaining sober can look unprofessional.

3. Shift the conversation to business talk at the appropriate time: It is best to focus on casual

conversation before your meal begins. Allow for casual conversation initially and make small talk with the other party. After a few minutes of small talk, introduce the topic at hand.

- When you begin the business talk is not always clear cut. However, a good rule of thumb is to stick to light personal topics until food and drinks have been ordered.

- Ask about the other party as much as you talk about yourself. Ask about your host's business endeavors, and show a genuine interest. If you're talking to someone from a different company, make sure to ask a lot of the company's culture, goals, and values. This is especially important if a business lunch is part of an interview process.

4. Silence your phone and put it away: Nowadays, phones seem to be attached to people's hips, but this is not at all appropriate while attending a business meal. Silence or turn your phone off before sitting down to eat and keep your phone concealed. You should avoid conducting business while at the table using your phone. Focus on the conversation and business being conducted at the table.

5. Handle the bill appropriately: When the bill comes, this can be uncomfortable. People feel awkward when it comes to money, tipping, and other aspects of payment. Whether you're paying or not, make sure to behave tactfully when the bill arrives.

- If you're paying the bill, make sure to tip well. Tipping adequately can say a lot about a person. A good rule of thumb is to tip between 20 and 25 percent.

- If you're paying the bill, only glance at the total. Try to keep your expression neutral. If there are any mistakes with the bill, deal with them after your guest has left.

- If the other party is paying, make sure to thank them for lunch before leaving. Send a follow-up email the next day, thanking them again.

6. Excuse yourself when leaving the table: If at any point you need to leave the table to use the restroom or take an important phone call, be sure to politely excuse yourself quietly and carefully. Do not abruptly leave the table and cause confusion, disruption or noise.

- Remember, when excusing yourself, place your napkin on the chair and not the table. Placing your napkin on the table signifies you're leaving the restaurant, while placing it on the chair signifies you'll be back momentarily.

Part 3. Following Basic Etiquette

1. Select a suitable meal choice: Be careful when ordering. You want to make sure you pick something that is appropriate in terms of price. You should also avoid anything too messy, as you do not want to make things awkward by struggling to handle your food.

- Try to get a sense of what others are ordering first and pick something within the same price range. You should not order lobster if your other guests are eating sandwiches or salads.

- If you're dining with a potential new boss or colleague, strive to match what he or she is ordering. You want to look like you fit in with the culture. If your boss is health conscious, for example, do not order a hamburger after he or she orders a caesar salad.

- Pick food that's easy to eat. You do not want to be struggling with a rack of ribs while you're trying to have a conversation. You should also avoid anything that produces a strong smell, as you don't want to do anything that could potentially annoy a co-worker, boss, or colleague.

2. Sit up straight and keep your elbows off the table: Proper table manners are key to making a good impression. Sit up nice and straight and don't slouch while at the table. Keep your hands in your lap or gently by your sides and avoid resting them on the table. These are very basic table manners, but you may forget them if you're nervous.

3. Begin eating once everyone has been served: When the food begins to come out, pay close attention and only start eating once you see everyone at the table has been served. It is considered rude to begin eating before everyone's food has arrived.

- You should also try to eat at roughly the same pace as your colleagues. Eating too fast or too slow can make others feel awkward.

4. Place your napkin in your lap and avoid talking with your hands while holding your silverware:

Make sure you put your napkin in your lap before consuming any food. If any food drops or you spill, you want to be sure your clothes are protected by your napkin. Additionally, while eating, try to avoid moving your hands a great deal or obnoxiously while holding your silverware.

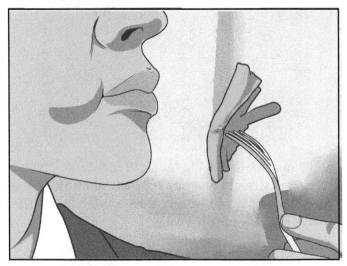

5. Chew with your mouth closed: This is an oldie but a goodie: make sure you never speak with food in your mouth and always chew with your mouth closed. You want to make sure you look polished and sophisticated while attending a business meal and this can be accomplished through simple table manners about chewing.

6. Place your fork and knife in the proper position once the meal is over: When the meal is over, you will want to signify to the waiter you are done eating. Take your fork and knife and place them in the four o'clock position. This means you place your fork and knife across your plate. If your plate were a clock, your fork and knife would be pointing to four. The knife should be above the fork, with the blade pointing inward.

- You should also place your napkin on the table next to your plate.

- Even while you're signifying your finished, wait staff usually ask if you're done out of courtesy. Smile and say, "Yes," and then thank the waiter for removing your plate.

How to Eat with Etiquettes

Steps

1. Sit up straight at the table. This will give people a good first impression. But try not to look stiff and nervous,this will put them on edge.

2. If you are served first, do not start eating until the other guests at you table are served too. Otherwise you will seem rude.

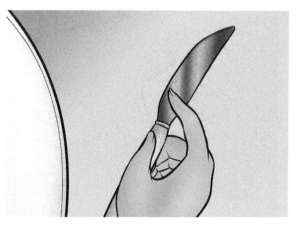

3. Hold the knife in the right hand.

4. To cut something,you stab your fork into it, but be careful and do this gently. Then while holding the food in place with the fork,cut of a small piece with your knife.

5. You can either hold the knife in your right hand or rest it on the edge of your plate,whichever you find more comfortable.

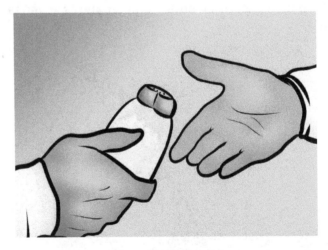

6. If you need something,do not reach across the table to get it. Ask politely the person sitting closest to the thing to hand it over to you.Example "Can you please hand me the salt?"

7. When you are finished, put your fork and knife in the middle of the plate side by side and wait till the waiter collects it. This means that you are finished and are ready to be served the next course.

8. When or if pouring drinks, ask the people do they want refills. If they do fill their glasses first, before filling your own.

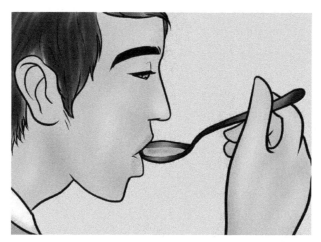

9. If eating soup, do not slurp. This is extremely rude and will make people uncomfortable.

10. When chewing keep your mouth closed,and do not talk until you swallow every last bite.

11. Do not wave your knife, fork, spoon etc. in the air while not using them. This could be dangerous to the person sitting next to you and may harm them. You will also seem rude.

12. When at a dinner keep your voice audible, but not loud.

13. When you burp or yawn, cover your mouth with your hand. No one really wants to see what's going on in your mouth.

14. Do not pick your nose. If you do you can be sure not to be invited to dinner ever again.

15. If you need to fart, excuse yourself to the bathroom. If you do it at the table, and it's loud and also stinks you will not get another invitation again.

Dining Etiquette in the Workplace

Not every business meeting takes place in an office or boardroom -- some may take place on the golf course or at a restaurant. Doing business over a meal, or just dining with a client or co-worker, can be stressful if you are unfamiliar with proper dining etiquette. Some businesses may even test potential employees' mettle by breaking bread during an interview. The best way to make a bad impression at a business meal is to slurp your soup or demonstrate some other lack of refinement and manners. Whether it costs you a contract or just makes you the butt of office jokes, failure to follow the rules when eating can be disastrous.

Before Eating

When you are involved in a business meal, you want to be sure to fit in with your dining companions and be appropriately respectful of your host. That means greeting fellow diners, waiting until the host sits down before seating yourself and standing when a senior executive or woman enters the room or arrives at the table. Start with small talk rather than launching straight into business. As far as ordering your meal, follow the host's lead in terms of what to order, and never order the most expensive item on the menu. Avoid messy foods or foods you need to eat with your hands.

If you have made a reservation at the restaurant, you must keep it and be on time. Also, remember to send a thank-you note when appropriate.

Utensils

Nothing trips up a diner like the array of utensils at a fancy meal. The safest rule is to use your forks, spoons and knives from the outside in, but if you dine at formal restaurants on a regular basis, learn to identify which utensil is used for which dish. Your napkin and forks are to the left of your dinner plate, and the forks follow the outside-in pattern: Use them for salad and then the meal, and if there is a third fork there, it is for dessert. On the right side of the plate, the large spoon is for soup, the smaller spoon is for tea or coffee and the knife is for cutting. Your butter knife is normally on the small bread plate -- and the plate to your left is yours. If a small spoon and fork are placed at the head of your plate, they are for dessert. Your glasses are to your right; from the outside in, they are for white wine, then red wine and then water. Always put your napkin on your lap when you sit, and fold it when you get up, don't just wad it into a ball.

While Eating

When you are eating in a working environment, basic table manners are always important. That means chewing with your mouth closed and not speaking while you are chewing, for starters -- and no elbows on the table. Proper form is to pass food items to the right, asking the person to your left if you would like something; remember to say "please" and "thank you." Tear rolls one bite at a time, and butter them accordingly, with butter you've placed in your own bread plate; slice entrees one bite at a time, as well. Avoid slurping and smacking while you eat, and place your used utensils on a plate rather than leaving them in a soup or salad bowl.

Eating at Your Desk

Sometimes, a working lunch means actually eating at your desk while you are on the job. When that is the case, keep nearby co-workers in mind while you dine and avoid food with strong odors, burning the microwave popcorn and leaving smelly food remnants in your garbage can. Particularly in a cubicle or shared-office environment, a powerful smell can be disruptive to neighbors. Don't eat in front of customers or during a meeting unless others are doing so.

How to Maintain Business Lunch and Dinner Etiquette

Part 1. Choosing the Location

1. Choose the place very carefully to show your respect to the partner. If you never been there before, check the place few days before the chosen date (comfort, suitability, smoking/non-smoking place/tables, terrace, menu suggestions etc.). In case of any doubts, consult the management.

Part 2. Arriving

1. Whether a female or not, the organizer shall arrive always first. If you arrive together and you are the organizer, you enter the door first (an old gesture: you are protecting your guest).

2. If the company is mixed, the inviter enters first (if a female, she shall be followed by the husband/

partner/senior manager of the company) then the ladies, after them the senior of men, other men, and the youngest is the last.

3. Men shall help the ladies by the wardrobe/cloakroom.

4. A nice gesture to draw the chair for the ladies, giving them a chance to seat first.

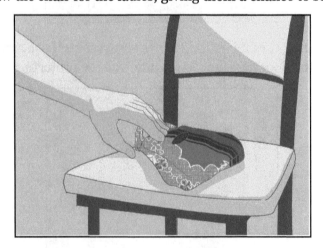

5. Place purses or clutches on a nearby unused chair. Do not place them on the tabletop. Never put them on the floor.

Part 3. Ordering

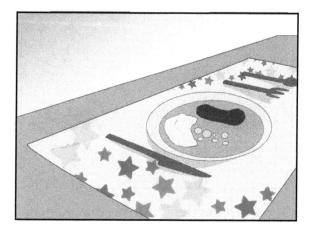

1. Choose food that won't create a mess. Remembering your attire, order something that will cause as little mess if it is spilled or dropped as possible. For example, women's attire with ruffles near the throat is not easy to keep clean.

2. Beware of food of any kind that cause gas. Do not partake.

3. Be frugal and sensible with your meal choices. Though it may be paid later by your company, do not splurge just because you can. Dessert is not needed unless the business you need to accomplish has not been finalized yet.

4. Order similar, if not exactly the same as they do, to ensure compatibility. Subduing your urge to get what you want is not as important as fitting in with the business at hand you need to master.

- Knowing if your business guests are vegetarians, vegans, or other dining preferences are will help in pre-planning your meal.

5. Encourage those from out of town to enjoy foods common in your part of the country. This makes for easy, casual conversation, though keep away from spicy foods.

6. Do not order hard liquor. A straight frame of mind is more important. However, a nice wine that complements the meal may be needed, though ask the others at the table their preference. Alternatively, order one on the fine dining list that is generally accepted.

- Knowledge beforehand of the type meal being served and pre-choosing the wine will impress the others dining with you.

Part 4. Conversing

1. Start with positive conversation. Positive points are to be introduced before the first course is served. Any negative conversation is to be handled quickly after the first course has mostly been consumed.

Part 5. Dining

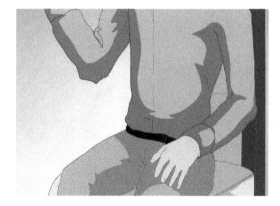

1. Keep the non-dominant hand in your lap at all times possible.

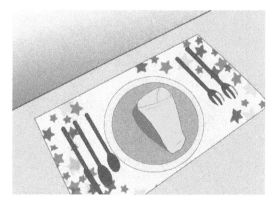

2. If confused about what utensil to use, start from the outside. Then work your way in for each dish served.

3. Use one hand to scoop up food only. Do this unless a knife is needed, in which case, use with the non-dominant hand only, then place the knife on the upper farthest angle of the plate after cutting.

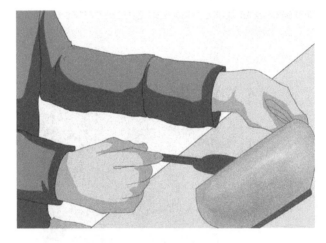

4. Tilt the soup or ice cream bowl gently away from body. Use a spoon to scoop up soup/cream and place in your mouth, then return the bowl to original position.

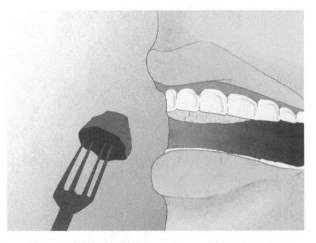

5. Keep all bites of food smaller than mouth size, for easy consumption.

How to use a Fork and Knife

Part 1. European (Continental) Style

1. Know that the fork is on the left side of the plate and the knife is on the right. If you have more than one fork, the outer one is your salad fork and the inner one is for your main dish. The fork for your main dish will be larger than your salad fork.

2. To cut into items on your plate, pick up and hold your knife in your right hand. The index finger is mostly straight and rests near the base of the top, blunt side of the blade. The other four fingers wrap around the handle. While your index finger is resting on the top, your thumb juxtaposes it on the side. The end of the knife handle should be touching the base of your palm.

- This is the same in both styles. And both styles cater to right-handers. If you're left-handed, consider reversing pretty much anything you read on this topic.

3. Hold your fork in your left hand. The tines (prongs) face away (downward) from you. The index finger is straight, and rests on the back-side near the head of the fork, but not so close you are in danger of touching the food. The other four fingers wrap around the handle.

- This is often referred to as the "hidden handle" method. This is because your hand is pretty much covering the entirety of the handle, secluding it from view.

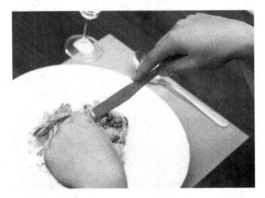

4. Bend the wrists, so that your index fingers are pointing down towards your plate. This makes the tip of the knife and fork also point towards the plate somewhat. Your elbows should be relaxed and not at all up in the air or uncomfortable.

- While we're at it, typically your elbows should be off the table at all times. But if you're taking a break from using your cutlery and in an informal setting, don't stress about it.

5. Hold the food down with the fork by applying pressure through the index finger. If you're cutting, place the knife close to the base of the fork and cut with a sawing motion. Foods like pasta will only

require a swift, easy cut, while chewy meats will take a bit of work. Generally, only cut one or two bites at a time.

- Hold the fork so the tines (prongs) are curving toward you, with the knife further away from you than the fork. At an angle is fine, too -- just make sure you can see your knife clearly to know where you're cutting. You should be able to look over your fork to your knife.

6. Bring smallish bits of food to your mouth with the fork. In this style of eating, bring the fork to your mouth with the tines curving downward. The back of the fork will be up as you bring it to your mouth.

- Keep the fork in your left hand, even if you're right-handed. You may find that this method is the more efficient of the two if you experiment with both.

Part 2. American Style

1. When cutting, hold the fork in your left hand. *Unlike* the Continental method, the American style of using a fork adopts more of a pen-like hold. The handle rests against your hand in between your thumb and forefinger, your middle finger and thumb are holding the base, and your index finger rests on top. Again, the tines are downward, curving away from you.

2. Only when cutting, place the knife in your right hand. This hand positioning is the same as in

the aforementioned style -- with your index finger along the base and your other fingers wrapped around it.

3. Make a cut. Hold the food down with your fork (tines down), cutting through with the knife in a gentle sawing motion. Your fork should be closer to you than your knife. Only cut one or two bites before continuing.

4. Now switch hands. Here comes the main difference between the two styles: after cutting a bite, put your knife down on the edge of your plate (blade at 12 o'clock, handle at 3 o'clock) and transfer your fork from your left hand to your right. Turn it so the tines are curving upward and take a bite.

- This is the method that was prevalent when America first became America. Europe used to use it, but has since moved on, favoring a more efficient approach. The jump hasn't quite made it across the pond, though there are pockets of difference everywhere.

5. Apart from cutting, eat with your fork in your right hand, tines facing upward. If you are eat-

ing a dish that doesn't require cutting, keep your fork in your right hand at all times with this method. Tines can face downward if you're taking a bite, but will generally return upward for the majority of the time. However, do know that only in the absolute most formal of settings will this ever be an issue. We're talking when the President is sitting across from you. Other than that, don't stress.

- Your silverware should never touch the table. If you're only using your fork, be sure your knife is resting along the edge of your plate. When you put your fork down, rest the handle on the edge, tines near the center of the plate.

Part 3. Dining Extras

1. Understand the table set-up. For 95% of meals, you'll probably just be dealing with a knife, fork and spoon. But for those fancy occasions, you may see a few more pieces and wonder what the heck you should be doing. Here's a rough outline:

- A four-piece setting is a knife, a salad fork, a place fork (main dish), a place knife, and a teaspoon for coffee. The salad fork will be on the outside and smaller than your place fork.

- A five-piece setting is all that and a soup spoon. The soup spoon will be much larger than your coffee teaspoon.

- A six-piece setting is a first-course fork and knife (on the outside), main course fork and knife, and a dessert/salad fork and coffee teaspoon. Those last two will be the small ones.

- A seven-piece setting is all that and a soup spoon. The soup spoon will be much larger than your coffee teaspoon and isn't a knife or a fork.

  ○ If you ever see a small fork on your right (forks generally never go on the right), it's an oyster fork.

  ○ Utensils are generally placed in the order of their use. When in doubt, start from the outside and work your way in.

2. When you're just pausing between bites, place your silverware in a resting position. There are two different ways to signify to your waiter that you aren't finished:

- European style: Cross your knife and fork on your plate, fork over knife, tines facing down. The two should form an upside-down "V."

- American style: The knife goes near the top of your plate, blade at 12 o'clock, handle at 3 o'clock. The fork is placed tines upward, just at a slight angle from your body.

3. When you're finished eating, place your silverware in a completed position. This lets your waiter know your plate can be cleared (if he's in the know, that is). Again, the two schools of thought are:

- European style: Knife and fork parallel to each other, handles at 5 o'clock, blade and tines in the center of your plate (tines downward).

- American style: The same as European style, only the tines of the fork are facing upward.

4. Get crafty with rice and other small items. You will need to pick them up by the fork in a slight scooping manner, rather than stabbing at them fruitlessly. The American style generally prefers to rely solely on the fork (again, less efficient), while the European style sometimes employs the help of the knife blade or a piece of bread for scooping.

5. To eat pasta, twirl it with your fork. If you have a spoon, ensnare a few noodles with your fork and twirl them, resting on the base of your spoon. If the noodles are too long and are proving cumbersome, you can cut them with your knife if need be. But before you take any drastic measures, just try taking only a few noodles at a time. And make sure you have a napkin at the ready.

- If you're not good with pasta, you are in good company. It's messy for even the most seasoned of pasta-eaters at times. It's less about the knife and fork and more about not slurping.

How to use a Napkin with Proper Table Etiquette

Steps

1. Put your napkin on your lap, right away. Once you have been seated by the host, the first and foremost thing you should do is pick up your napkin and without flicking it violently, unfold it and place it comfortably on your lap. This is its home until either you need to go to the restroom, or the meal has finished.

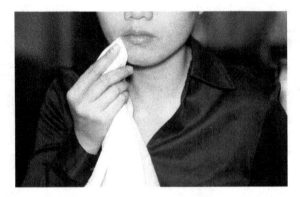

2. Wipe your mouth with care. During the meal, it will be customary that you will need to wipe your mouth at certain promptings. To wipe your mouth, gently dab your mouth and allow the napkin to soak residue from the area. It is also vital that you use your napkin before sipping your wine or other beverage, so you don't leave any greasy mouth excess on the lip of the glass.

3. Do not use it as a handkerchief. At no stage during the meal should you use your napkin like a

tissue as a means to blow your nose. Simply excuse yourself from the table if you need to, and visit the bathroom instead.

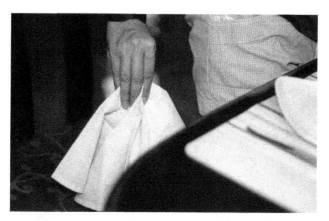

4. Be careful when you get up. If you do need to take a trip to the restroom during the meal, excuse yourself from the table and place your napkin neatly on the lap of your seat (not the arm or the top) until you return. Never place it back onto the table during the meal.

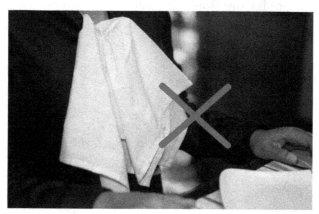

5. Never wear your napkin like a cravat. Toddlers wear bibs, not adults.

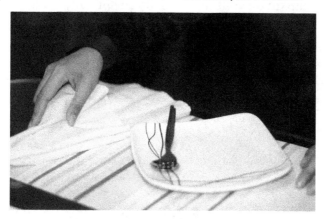

6. Wrap up at the end of the meal. The host should signal that you have reached the end of the meal by placing his or her napkin on the table beside the plate (never on it). It is fine for you to mimic this gesture and at the same time thank them for a wonderful meal if you can.

How to Eat Soup Politely

Steps

1. Be seated at the table. If you are eating soup on the couch or somewhere else, be sure to use a Stable Table™ or a tray, to prevent it from slopping around and making a mess, or from burning you.

2. Place your serviette or napkin on your lap in case you spill anything.

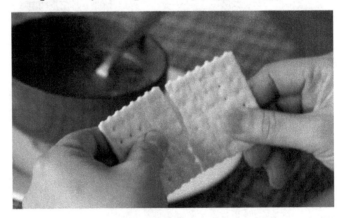

3. Break up any bread or bread roll on the side plate next to you and eat it intermittently with the soup.

4. Pull the dish close to you to make sure you don't spill the soup while eating.

5. Have the correct spoon. A soup spoon is the best spoon to eat soup. Failing that, use a spoon larger than a teaspoon but smaller than a serving dish spoon.

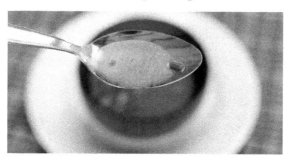

6. Fill the spoon about three-quarter the way full. Do not overfill a soup spoon or it will spill as you lift it. Lift your spoon carefully and slowly from the bowl to your mouth.

7. Continue eating soup in this manner, methodically, slowly and with care. Always place the entire spoon into your mouth to prevent the need to slurp. Be careful not to clank it on your teeth.

8. As you near the end of the soup, tilt the bowl away from you and not towards you. This is considered the polite way to finish soup as there is much less risk of spilling the soup into your lap.

9. Rest the spoon in your bowl at the end and push the bowl away from you gently.

How to Chew with your Mouth Closed

Steps

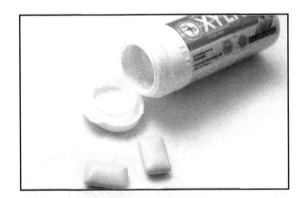

1. Practice with chewing gum. Close your mouth and chew with your back teeth. Use one or two sticks of gum for this practice. Remember to breathe through your nose, not through your mouth.

2. Start out with small portions of food; first soft food, like ice-cream or yogurt. Put a little bit of the food into your mouth. Now close your mouth, chewing with only your back teeth. Chew slowly; this helps you keep your mouth closed.

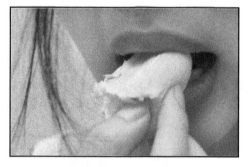

3. Once you have mastered it with the soft foods, try chewing larger portions at a time, as you would normally eat. This is no reason to open your mouth. Still chew with it closed.

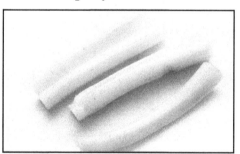

4. Move on to the more solid foods now, like fruits, rice, and bread. Follow the same principle: small portions at first, then slowly work your way up. Chew slowly.

5. Once you are past this stage, try the hardest foods, such as granola bars and cereals. While these may make noise, it is no excuse to open your mouth while chewing.

How to Avoid Spilling

Steps

1. Walk slowly. Scientists have found that a cup of coffee just happens to be the right size to set up waves when we walk. The faster one walks, the quicker and stronger the waves. You know what happens next—flying coffee. By walking slower, the sympathetic resonances are decreased, and your drink stays where it belongs.

2. Look at your drink. Keep your eye on your drink, not your feet. This not only helps you walk slower, by focusing on your drink you are constantly aware and making adjustments for any sloshing that's going on.

3. Don't rush. The slower you start moving, the less the drink in your cup will start sloshing. By

not dashing from here to there, you make it easier to keep your drink in the cup, and not on the ground. Be alert for others in the area, since a bump or even a close call can result in an accident.

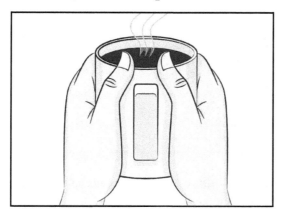

4. Hold the cup or plate with both hands. This makes it easier to control. Make several trips instead of trying to carry a plate in one hand and a glass in the other.

5. Don't carry drinks on an empty stomach. Have a snack, or drink some juice and eat some fruit if you are going to an event where you're to have food. Holding anything on an empty stomach can be extra difficult.

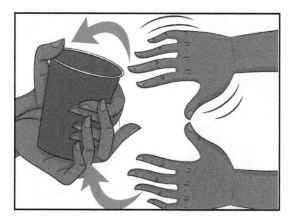

6. Know which hand is steady and for what things. If you're using one hand to carry a beverage, use your steady hand. If you're using two hands, use the steady hand to control the sloshing, and the other hand as support.

7. Know your limits. Soup is nearly impossible to carry on a cafeteria tray if you have a hand tremor. Avoid it or soak a piece of bread in it.

8. Carry a cafeteria tray with one forearm under the tray. Your forearm can be much steadier than your hands. Also, either avoid putting tall drinks on a cafeteria tray or hold both the tray and the drink with one of your hands

How to React when you Spill Someone's Drink

Steps

1. Avoid letting the situation happen in the first place. You are most likely to spill someone's drink

when you are making magnanimous gestures, carrying a few drinks of your own, or if you are feeling buzzed. So remember to be observant at these high risk moments. If you do spill someone's drink, do not ignore it, but act quickly to assess the situation and defuse any hostile vibrations.

2. Apologize. If you have just spilled someone's drink, you should apologize immediately and unreservedly. If they are a decent type, this should stop them from getting too agitated.

3. Considering buying a replacement. Have a look at the damage. If you have just knocked their drink out of their hands all over the floor, then you need to replace it immediately. If you've only knocked an ounce of beer or two from the top of their glass, then it shouldn't be a big deal.

- Most people will be okay about it, and no replacement drink should be required. If they become confrontational, it would be best just to buy them a drink to save you the trouble.

How to Stir a Beverage Noiselessly

Steps

1. Take the spoon between the thumb and forefinger.

2. Insert the spoon in the middle of the of the cup until the entire head is submerged.

3. Fix your gaze on the rim of the cup opposite yourself and place your ring finger along the edge of the cup. (Measure the width of a finger and a half with your ring and middle fingers.) Move the spoon until the center touches your fingers.

4. Try again without using your finger. Then, try the same action in the other direction.

5. Draw an imaginary circle in the cup and move the spoon following this imaginary path.

6. Remove your fingers and try it without help. Remember that the imaginary path is a "safe" circle where you can move the spoon as you wish. Outside it, it's quite certain that you'll hear the sound you are trying to avoid.

7. Practice. The trick is to move the wrist and the fingers rather than the whole arm. Practicing will ensure that you master this art quickly.

Dress Code for Workplace

Clothing regulations vary from one workplace to the other. Dress codes are generally set in the workplace for aesthetic recognition, or to look appropriate to their responsibilities. Dress codes may also regulate the use of jewelry and hats. This chapter examines professional dress code, business casual and corporate dressing.

Corporate Dressing for Success at Workplace

Every organization expects its employees to be well groomed and presentable. Employees need to understand that sensible dressing goes a long way in building their professional image. As an employee, you are also representing your organization. One needs to be formally dressed to make a powerful first impression at the workplace. First impressions are indeed extremely crucial. If you do not dress well, getting hired by a reputed organization could be a challenge. Even if you get selected, you would find difficulties in winning respect and appreciation of others. Credentials are essential but appearances count as well. Trust me; it would be difficult for you to impress a client if you are not formally dressed.

Corporate dressing helps you climb the ladder of success in the shortest possible time frame. People around you will speak high of you even if you are not around. Employees are the lifeline of every organization. They are the ones who either make or break an organization. Even the best of machinery would not help, if the employees do not strive hard to deliver their level best. The moment employees start treating their work as a mere source of burden, their performance drops down drastically, eventually affecting the productivity of organization. One does not feel like working if he/she is not smartly dressed.

Corporate dressing makes you feel confident and fresh throughout the day. The moment you put on your formal clothes, you tend to be alert and attentive at work. Corporate Dressing inculcates a sense of pride and team spirit among employees, one of the most essential factors which decide the growth chart of an individual.

An employee who does not adhere to the dress code of his/her organization often gets ignored by his fellow workers and senior management. He/she is often not invited for important business meetings, presentations, seminars or conferences. Jeans, T-shirts, sneakers, heavy jewellery are not at all accepted at workplaces. Don't be surprised if you are denied entry to office because you are wearing a T shirt on a Monday. Every organization has a dress code and it is your moral responsibility to follow the same. If you do not dress according to your work culture, it simply shows your irresponsible and careless attitude.

It is essential for employees to make a mark of his/her own at the workplace. Corporate dressing helps you get noticed and stand apart from the rest. You need to create your own unique style to survive the fierce competition. Why would your boss pick you for an important business deal if there is no difference between you and your team member? Dressing formally gives you that extra edge over your fellow workers at the workplace. If you are not sensible towards your dressing, believe me you will remain a team member throughout your life. It may sound bitter, but it is actually true. As a manager, you need to be a source of inspiration for others. What do you think your team members would wear if you yourself attend office in Jeans and T shirts? Do you expect them to wear formals? Ask yourself.

Corporate dressing makes you a role model for others in organization. You sort of become their fashion icon.

Employees who dress well are not only appreciated by their internal staff but also by clients and external parties. Do not wear just anything and come to work. Do not give an impression that someone has forcefully sent you to work. Corporate dressing goes a long way in developing a pleasing personality- a must in organizations.

Corporate dressing helps you earn brownie points at workplace and pushes you to the top slot in a short span of time.

How to Dress Professionally

Dressing professionally is vital for success in an office or academic environment. Your appearance makes a statement on your professionalism, and showing up in sloppy or inappropriate attire can kill a career. Although what constitutes as 'professional' varies from office to office, there are a few key style guidelines to follow.

Part 1. Determining the Level of Formality of Your Workplace

1. Always dress to match the workplace setting. Some workplaces will provide a written dress code outlining specifically what is appropriate and what is not. For others, you may have to judge based on what others there are wearing.

- Formal Business attire is typically the dress code used for high-profile jobs: government officials, managing workers, lawyers, and so on. It is also for businesses which cultivate formality, such as credit unions. Be aware some businesses dress formally most days, but have "casual Friday" or will otherwise relax the rules for certain reasons or occasions (such as a walk-a-thon, fundraiser, or if the air conditioning breaks down).

- "Business casual" is the term often used for less formal (but not *informal*) office environments. Be aware that this varies by culture, region, and profession. Sometimes "business casual" offices will become "business formal" for important occasions, such as a press conference, a high-profile visitor arriving, or an important seminar.

- "Black tie" is typically only used only for very specific and special events, (such as awards dinners, formal banquets, or galas.) These typically require a tuxedo for men and an evening gown for women.

- Typically, the higher paying the position, the higher your rank, the more professionally your office clothing should be. (However, note this is not universal--the CEO of a software company may dress far less formally than an intern at a law firm.)

- Some jobs have a specific uniform. For instance, a chef, nurse, life guard, judge, or police officer. This is a professional dress code, but usually this needs very little further discussion.

2. Know your Office Culture. Making professional dress even more confusing is the fact that types of work environment make a big difference in what one wears. Although you are usually fine following guidelines as discussed, realize that workplaces may encourage a certain "look" that goes beyond simple "Office Formal" or "Business Casual" definitions. This usually has to do with what the company makes, sells, or provides.

- An African aid organization, for instance, may encourage people to dress in clothes made in Africa and sold on its website in order to promote awareness and fair trade.

- The athletic department of a university may be much more accepting of athletic clothing such as running shoes.

- Highly artistic or creative workplaces may allow a lot more leeway in the way of dress. A fashion-based office may have much different expectations of dress than an accounting firm.

3. Factor in the season--sometimes. Professional dress code in much of the world has some seasonality, based partially on the weather but also on seasonal styles. But be aware that some regions do not really have changes in clothing based on seasons. (Such as the tropics). But for areas with clothing seasons, many areas the following rules of thumb apply:

- Linen, seersucker, and madras cloth tend to be appropriate for summer only.

- Wool clothing tends to be for fall and winter only.

- In America, an old saying is "no white after Labor Day"...which used to refer to white linen fabrics used a lot in summer dresses rather than absolutely no white whatsoever. This is a very outdated rule. Feel free to brazenly wear a white shirt in the office in winter.

- Layers of appropriate clothing can help negotiate in-between seasons, when temperatures can fluctuate. For instance, a cardigan can be useful coming into work on a crisp fall day, and removed later when it warms up. A pair of warm leggings can allow you to wear skirts comfortably in winter.

- Keep in mind that the amount of visible skin allowable will be slightly different in business settings. What is acceptable in one culture may be unacceptable in another. For instance, what is fine for a women in France may be too revealing in Qatar.

- If you choose to remove layers of clothing, make sure you are in no way being revealing or inappropriate about the skin you choose to show. If you are wearing a camisole under a blazer, and you are not supposed to have a sleeveless shirt, you may be out of luck.

4. Know what colors to wear. No color is completely "off limits" but it is more formal and professional

stick mainly with a neutral color palette. Formal business suits for both men and women tend to be black, brown, gray, tan, or navy blue. Shirts tend to be lighter in color, with white, off-white, and light shades of colors.

- This limited color palette may sound boring and dull at first. However, it also can create a wardrobe that allows for many items to interchange easily. Basing a wardrobe around black, white, and khaki will assure that everything goes with just about everything.

- "Pops" of color with accessories such as ties, shoes, and scarves are typically fine, but, it is safer to go with subtle rather than bright and bold.

- Multi-colored shirts can be acceptable, such as a classic striped Oxford-style shirt.

- These guidelines are for people who need to make their dress more professional. Brighter and more varied colors can be entirely appropriate, depending on the occupation, and the overall appearance of the outfit. But if you are unsure or inexperienced, select conservative colors--they are perennial office clothes favorites because they always look right.

5. Pay attention to those around you. If you are unsure exactly how formal or casually to dress, try looking at the clothing choices of those in your profession, at your office, or attending the same event as you.

- In general, it is better to be slightly overdressed than it is to be under-dressed.

- If you are not able to get a good glimpse or have a chat with someone in your field, try searching images on the internet for people in similar positions in the company or last year's event. Pay attention to the appearance of people in these images, and dress accordingly.

- Be careful of events that may require a dramatic wardrobe change. For instance, at a conference, you may be required to wear suits and ties for the presentation. At the poolside cocktail receptions afterwards, swimsuits, Hawaiian shirts, and flip-flops are the garb of choice.

6. Remember good grooming. A great outfit will only get you so far. If you are lacking personal hygiene or have a bad haircut, you will not look professional. Make sure that you treat your entire appearance, (including hair, skin, and hygiene), with the same professional care as you do with your clothing.

- Shower. How often varies with culture, weather, and activity level. In most of America, at least every other day.

- Use deodorant.

- Make sure your hair is tidy and well-groomed.

- Facial hair (if any) should be trimmed and tidy. Stubble is not generally acceptable. "uni-brow" eyebrows or very heavy eyebrows are often considered unattractive in many areas.

- For women, legs should either be shaved or bare legs covered.

- Good oral hygiene matters. Be sure your breath has no noticeable odor. This is particularly important if you smoke or eat pungent food.

- Makeup for women should generally be restrained, according to culture.

Part 2. Dressing Business Formal

1. Know that formal business attire is tailored, conservative clothing. Although fashion changes

the little details, the essential core of formal office attire has really not changed much in decades. Dressing business formal is in some ways easier than in business casual, because the parameters are a lot narrower and well-defined. Both genders are typically expected to wear suits, typically in neutral colors (as described above). In general, men and women wear the following:

- For men: Formal suit, dress shirt, dress shoes, tie. Sometimes dressy slacks and sport coat are acceptable alternatives for a business suit. Often a shirt without an outer garment is acceptable.

- For women: business suit with skirt, blazer, blouse, dress shoes. Pants are also acceptable. A conservative dress may be substituted for a suit.

2.Pick your strong suit. Suits should be tailored for fit. Solid colors or pinstripes, and in good condition. Skirt suits should be knee-length and not too tight.

3. Choose the right tops. Shirts should be typically solid or pinstriped, tailored for fit, laundered, and ironed if required.

- Long sleeves are always more formal.

- Short sleeves are typically acceptable for spring and summer. However, some workplaces and cultures frown on bare arms.

- Women typically should steer away from sleeveless shirts if unsure if they are accepted or not. In some regions sleeveless shirts (but not one with straps, such as halter tops) are considered perfectly acceptable. In others, they are not considered appropriate. Tank tops, camisoles, tube tops, strapless tops amd "spaghetti strap" tops are not office formal clothing.

- Men should match shirt to tie.

- Women have to be extra careful in the cut and fit of office tops. Put bluntly, (especially for full-figured women) the bustline must be fitted properly so that it is not too revealing, too tight, or otherwise exposing more of the breasts so it is inappropriate. If your blouse gaps at the buttons of the bustline, the shirt does not fit you properly. Fabric or "fashion" tapes can be purchased to hold blouses in the right position.

4. Choose your ties carefully, men. Ties can allow for some color and pattern in an outfit that would be rather drab. It attracts attention, so be very careful in what you choose. Not all ties are appropriate for business formal dress code.

- Opt for either solid color, or have a small (no larger than a quarter) sized print that covers them.

- Avoid ties that have more than 3-4 colors total, and which have an image or scene printed onto them.

- Ties should match both your shirts and your suits and make sure they use colors that match or go with the rest of your outfit.

- Try to buy shirts and ties together, if possible. Men's stores coordinate colors to try to make the buying process easy. It may not be the same colors next year or even next season. If in doubt, ask for help--a good quality store will be happy to help you.

- Bow ties are also generally considered acceptable. However, they are far less common and can be considered unusual or "quirky".

- Bolo ties are often regionally acceptable in areas of the American South, Southwest, and West coast. However, they may or may not be considered an acceptable replacement for a tie depending on the workplace.

5. Say yes to the dress, ladies: Dresses can easily be worn in a business formal setting, but be careful with your selection. Choose dresses that are knee-length or longer, and are in a subtle print or solid color. Dresses should not be too tight-fitting and should not be revealing/ have a plunging neckline.

- A good blazer or suit jacket can make a dress more formal and versatile. This sort of outfit is the basis of the classic "day to night" women's wear, in which a woman goes to work wearing an evening appropriate dress coordinated with a work appropriate blazer. At the evening rendezvous, put aside the blazer for a less formal look.

6. Choose the right shoes for the job. Business formal jobs all require quality footwear, typically made of leather (or similar high-quality material).

- Men should always wear formal shoes, often in the baroque or oxford style.Lace up is more traditional.There are many slip-on loafers that also may be appropriate and formal. Black is the go-to color, although brown is sometimes acceptable.

- Women should typically wear low or moderate high heel shoes or flat pumps. Conservative boots are sometimes appropriate. Make sure details and embellishments are restrained. Women generally have more choice in color, but sticking to black and neutral colors is still safer.

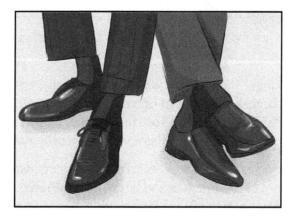

7. Sock it to them. In a formal office, white cotton athletic socks are usually not acceptable. If you are wearing socks, they should usually be dark (black is typical). Ideally they go with the pants or shoes.

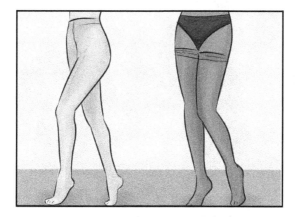

8. Women, wear your nylons. In a formal workplace, you should usually wear pantyhose, or tights under your skirt. Choose sheer tights in a neutral color.

- Leggings are not appropriate in a formal workplace; choose opaque tights instead.

- Barelegged (although well groomed) is becoming more acceptable. But if in doubt, put on a pair of pantyhose or tights.

9. Add other accessories. To complete your outfit, remember some accessories. In general, keep

jewelry and other accessories subtle and tasteful. Be careful of wearing too much, although what constitutes "too much" will vary from culture to culture. Also, what is OK for a man and a woman may be different. For instance:

- For men: cuff links, rings (such as a class or wedding ring), watch, pocket square (very formal). Necklaces and bracelets are often uncommon but usually acceptable if in good taste. Medical Alert jewelry is always OK. Most formal offices will not look favorably on body piercings, including earrings. Belt buckles should generally not be oversized.

- For women: Jewelry (rings, necklaces, earrings, bracelets, watches) are all typically acceptable, but be careful of too much or too large pieces. Pierced ears are almost universally OK (with studs or small earrings), generally other body piercings should not be visible. Scarves, belts, headbands, hair accessories (such as barrettes), are also all fine.

Part 3. Dressing Business Casual

1. Avoid the "Business Casual Don'ts". This is less formal and casual than traditional business guidelines. Unfortunately, it is often poorly defined and can be greatly different from one business to another. For instance, one business will be fine with Hawaiian print shirts with collars, while another will consider it too casual despite the collar. However, in general, the following are usually frowned upon:

- Jeans: especially ones with tears, stains, patches, or embellishments such as studs.

- Tank tops: especially spaghetti-strap styles.

- Shorts: Sometimes more tailored styles are acceptable--such as ones that resemble full length khakis, but shorter. Athletic styles are usually not OK.

- Informal T-shirts: Usually collared polo-type T-shirts are acceptable, or ones with shaping. If in doubt, do not go with *any* graphic images on your shirts. Shirts usually should not have elements which could be controversial or unacceptable--such as references to alcohol, sex, or violence. Avoid novelty T-shirts, (such as ones with cartoon characters) as this may come off as immature.

- Mini-skirts: Skirts should be no higher than about two inches above the knee.

- Plunging neckline: Be sure your V-neck shirt is not revealing too much, or your blouse buttoned too low.

- Keep it clean and tidy. Never come into work with clothes that are dirty, stained, ripped, or wrinkled (the one exception for wrinkled may be if that is part of the look, such as a seersucker shirt or crinkle cotton skirt).

2. Know the definite "Office Casual Do's":

- For men and women alike, business casual typically consists of a clean, pressed button-up shirt and a pair of neutral (such as khaki) slacks. Look for styles such as:

- Polo-style shirts: This collared shirt is the quintessential "office casual" choice for both men and women. Usually it will be available in a solid or striped. It can sometimes be found with a geometric pattern.

- Oxford-style shirt: This is acceptable in formal office clothing as well - a well-tailored shirt always looks good whether with khakis or a business suit.

- Tailored T-shirt: Some workplaces are fine with T-shirt style tops, as long as they are not informal T-shirts. For instance, a T-shirt with a classic scoop or crew neckline on a woman.

- Product shirts. In an office-casual workplace, often shirts given to you by your company or products that your company sells are acceptable. For instance, if you work at a company that sells outdoor equipment, wearing your company's shirts may be acceptable. But be careful--just because your company sells tank tops may not make it OK to wear tanks tops to your accounting job.

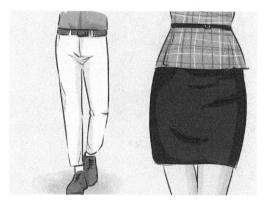

3. Choose the right bottoms: Find a few pairs of black, navy blue, khaki, or brown pants. In "office casual" the pants are usually cotton and can be a little more "relaxed" than those found in formal offices. Woman can wear skirts into the mixed in the same aforementioned color palette.

- Avoid patterns if you are unsure on what looks professional. There are great, classic patterns such as pinstripe that look great on pants, but it is easy to make a mistake.

- Generally avoid wearing white pants or a skirt. While entirely appropriate, these items can stain easy, if you spill your tea you may be out of luck.

- A patterned skirt can be appropriate for women. Try a small floral or geometric print.

4. Select a few jackets or sweaters. It will inevitably get chilly, so make sure you have the right items for cold weather. Men can choose to wear a cardigan, sweater, or sports coat over the top of their button up shirt for a smart look. Women can wear layered sweaters, cardigans, and structured jackets and blazers to good effect. When desired/necessary, a pashmina or cashmere scarf can be worn for added warmth and style.

5. Consider wearing dresses (for women). Dresses are sometimes appropriate in a business casual setting, so long as they follow a few basic guidelines. Dresses should be knee-length or longer,

expose no skin below the collarbone, and mostly cover the shoulders. Small patterns and solid colors work best, and can be accessorized for added visual interest. Throw on a cardigan or matching jacket for layering in cooler weather.

6. Pick the right shoes. Business casual offices vary widely in shoe choice, based on the type of environment. Some good guidelines:

- Close-toed shoes. Sandals are usually a no-no. Flip-flops are a definite "no". Women can wear flats or heels, but they must be in good condition and quality. In general, stick to neutral colored shoes and stay away from bold patterns.

- Be careful of really, really casual shoes. Even if it is closed-toe, some shoes usually do not belong in a professional environment. For example, high top Converse sneakers are best left to teenagers. The classic "Croc" shoe is much too casual for most professional workplaces.

Part 4. Avoiding Common Mistakes

1. Do not shop at the junior's department for work clothes. If you are old enough to have to consider

professional clothing, do so where grown-ups shop. That also goes for clothing stores that cater exclusively to teens and very young adults like "Forever 21". That does not necessarily mean you have to dress exactly like your mother or father. However, if you are trying to find clothing to help you to be taken seriously as a young adult, you have to accept that you have to dress the part--at least at work.

2. Shop at stores with high customer service: In putting together a wardrobe of work clothes, often your best ally are good salespeople in a quality store. This can be a stand-alone store, such as a menswear store, or a department store. A knowledgeable salesperson can help you select clothing to meet your needs, be sure it fits properly, and accessorize appropriately.

- Try to find a salesperson dressed more or less in the way you want to dress. This may be a good indication that he or she has a fashion sensibility that matches yours. However, be open for other individuals. That matronly salesperson may actually really know what the young people like these days.

- It can help to bring someone whose judgement you trust to this sort of shopping trip.For instance, your mother or your fashion-savvy friend.

- Yes, you need to try on the clothes. Ill-fitting clothes are not professional, and fit cannot typically be judged well on a hanger. If ordering online, be prepared to send back things that do not fit.

- Make sure of fit. Just because you can wear it does not mean it fits properly. This includes pants that are showing the lines of your underwear, and baggy oversized shirts.

- Minor alterations are usually available at higher-end stores, and can make a great different in fit and appearance.

- Remember: the salesperson will ultimately sell you whatever you want, even if it really is not in line with appropriateness or good taste. Be sure that you keep your goal in sight, and not revert to great clothing that cannot be worn to work.

3. Be careful with jeans. To most of the world, blue jeans are a simple "no-no" in the workplace; they are considered appropriate for manual labor or leisure. However, America has *some* office-casual workplaces that are fine with jeans in the office. Before wearing your blue jeans to the office, really be sure it is OK with management. If in doubt, do not bring them to the office. Generally, however, non-ripped and un-embellished, dark wash jeans are better.

4. Keep your accessories to a minimum. Although accessorizing can be fun, piling on too many accessories can give a messy presentation.

- One accessory should usually be the focus.

- An old but still useful rule: Accessorize, but before leaving the house, take one item off.

- In general, wear a single necklace, pair of earrings, and one ring per hand at any time.

- Only a single bag or briefcase (never a fanny pack.) should be brought to work.

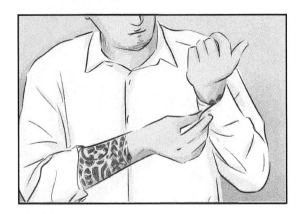

5. Try to cover up body modifications. Although not all offices advertise a preference for clear-skinned individuals, most workplaces expect employees to be as natural as possible. If you have large tattoos in obvious places or body piercings outside the ears, it may be necessary to slightly adjust your clothing to cover them. There is nothing wrong with having these things, but according to traditional dress code, they shouldn't be shown when you're on the clock.

6. Keep your clothes in good condition. Make sure you always wear clothes that are clean and pressed, or else give the impression of poor hygiene. Practice setting out your outfit the night before you wear it, so you are not at a loss for what to wear.

- Do your laundry once a week and ironing when necessary so that you do not deplete your arsenal of clean clothing and be forced to wear dirty clothes.

7. Do not repeat outfits within in the same week. Whether you are running late and just head to

your go-to outfit, or you just really love an outfit, avoid wearing the same exact outfit in a seven-day work period.

- Mixing and matching pieces is important and maximizes the usefulness of your wardrobe.

- Try practicing the two-week rule, where you only wear an outfit (where every piece is being repeated) only once in a two-week period.

8. Make sure your clothing "plays well together". Having all the right wardrobe pieces is great, but if they do not coordinate, they are essentially useless.

- Be sure to have more "basic" pieces than "statement" pieces. You will get more use out of certain items that will go with practically everything. There is nothing wrong with more flashy pieces, but they tend to not go with as many items.

- Try to buy items at the same store at the same time. Many store have clothing lines that are to be made in similar colors, patterns, and design. You are more likely to find coordinated outfits this way.

- As long as you match all your neutrals and add in a pop of color, you are likely be in good shape.

9. Keep a back-up outfit at work. If possible, have clothing that you can change into if there is a mishap at work. A shirt and bottom (such as pants or a skirt), shoes and a tie can be a lifesaver if

you get caught in the rain or someone spills something on you. This is also a good use of clothing that may not be your favorites, but are appropriate and fit you all right.

10. Do not wear anything that your boss or other superior will frown on. Your right to dress how you want in large part stops at the office door. This can mean that even if your clothes technically fit a dress code or guideline, your superiors can veto your apparel choice and to a large extent, *there is very little you can do about it*. This is not high school, where coming to school with an objectionable T-shirt just gets you to have to turn in inside-out.

- Issues such as head-scarves for religious reasons may or may not be legally protected in your country or state.

- Laws against sexual discrimination or inequality can also offer some protection, again depending on your area.

How to Dress Business Casual

Business casual is a term used to describe a type of office dress code or clothing style that is a little more casual than traditional business wear. Many employers adopt this dress code in an effort to allow employees to feel more comfortable on the job and to have more freedom of expression through their choice of attire. Although business casual is casual, it also doesn't mean that anything goes.

Method 1. Learning your Company's Policy

1. Ask for specific expectations. If you're not sure what your company's policy is, ask the HR rep. Dress more conservatively on the first day if you have no other coworkers to benchmark your attire against.

- Business casual is often thrown out there to describe how your employer thinks you should dress at work. The problem is that the expectations of individual companies often differ. For example, one company might want you to dress in business attire, minus a suit coat and tie, while another company may encourage you to wear khakis or jeans. When you are told to dress business casual, it is best to ask for details. Ask if your employer has an employee handbook that more clearly delineates the company's business casual policy.

2. Observe other employees. Look around and see what the other employees are wearing; this is a good gauge of what your employer expects when they say business casual.

3. Dress formally for interviews. If you're going on an interview and you don't know what your interviewer expects you to wear, the standard is business formal. Remember, it's better to be over-dressed than underdressed.

- Those who are interviewing for a job in business, banking and wealth management, politics, academia, engineering, or health sectors should dress business formal unless otherwise instructed.

- If no clothing type is specified, and the company you're interviewing for is outside the sectors listed above, stick with business casual.

Method 2. Business Casual for Women

1. Remember that skirts and dresses are acceptable as long as the hem falls just above the knees.

- As with men, black and grey are more formal, making for a safer bet.

- Avoid low-cut dresses or those with high slits.

- Avoid dresses (especially) and skirts that are more skin-tight.

- No sundresses.

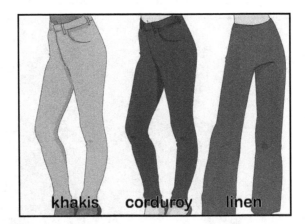

2. Opt for pants such as khakis, corduroy pants, linen pants or dress pants.

- No jeans, unless otherwise noted. If jeans are allowed by your employer, distressed jeans, jeans with holes, and "boyfriend" jeans are not desirable choices.

- Neutral colors are best.

3. Choose from a variety of shirts. Women have a few more options in this department than the men. Opt for conservative and not too revealing. Blouses, plain shirts, cotton shirts, sweaters, turtlenecks, vests, and sleeveless shirts are all acceptable.

- Tucked-in or untucked can both go, depending on the shirt.

- Unusual patterns are acceptable, as long as they are not wild. The standard, however, is a monotone shirt.

- Use a collar for a more formal look, and collarless shirts for a less formal look.

4. Try footwear such as leather shoes, flat trouser shoes, high heels; no open toed shoes. Avoid flip flops, sandals and sneakers.

- Heels are okay, so long as they aren't too conspicuous.

5. Complete the business casual look. Remember dress socks or pantyhose (with skirts or dresses)

and tastefully accessorize with light jewelry and a simple purse.

6. Check the list. Ask yourself the following set of questions if you're still not sure whether your outfit is acceptable.

- Would I wear this clubbing? The answer should be 'no.'

- Would I wear this to sleep? The answer should be 'no.'

- Would I wear this to do yard work? The answer should be 'no.'

- Would I wear this to a costume party? The answer should be 'no.'

Method 3. Business Casual for Men

1. Choose shirts that have collars, such as long-sleeve button down shirts. Always tuck the shirt in and pair the shirt with an appropriate belt. For business casual, tie is optional.

- White button-down shirts are the most formal and therefore the safest. Unlike pants, all manner of shirt colors are acceptable: Purple, pink, yellow, blue, and red.

- Choose shirts (and pants) in "formal" fabric: Cotton is king, and comes in many different flavors. Wool is acceptable, if itchy. Silk, rayon, and linen are frowned upon.

- Choose shirts in "formal patterns: Oxford, plaid, and poplin are a little less formal, but perfectly acceptable. Twill, herringbone, and broadcloth patterns are more formal and nice to use if sprucing up. Hawaiian and other irregular patterns are considered too casual.

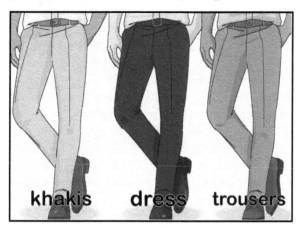

2. Wear pants styles such as khakis, dress pants, trousers and corduroy pants. Jeans are not considered business casual.

- Pleated pants and dark colors are more formal, conservative choices. If you want to be on the safe side, *over*dressing is less frowned upon than underdressing.

- Pants should extend to the top of your shoe, or slightly longer. Pants that don't reach down to your shoe are considered high-water pants; pants that fold and bunch up near the feet are considered too baggy.

- Avoid pants in loud colors such as red, yellow, and purple. Camouflage is not allowed, neither are white pants — they feel a little too informal for even business casual. Stick with black, brown, grey, khaki, dark blue and dark green pants.

3. Consider pairing your shirt with a sweater or sweater vest. V-neck sweaters work best if wearing a a collar.

- Turtlenecks can be worn in combination with a blazer for a sleek look and a little bit of novelty.

- If you want to wear a suit coat and still look business casual, dress it down with khakis instead of suit pants.

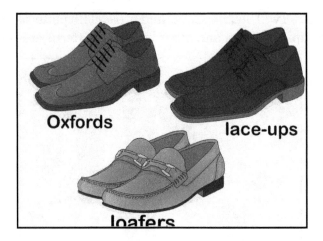

Oxfords — lace-ups — loafers

4. Select formal leather shoes, and don't forget the dress socks. Stick to black, brown, or grey shoes. Oxfords, lace-ups, and loafers are all standards.

List of Dont's:

- Sneakers, sandals, flip-flops or other open-toed shoes.
- Sports shirts, sweat-shirts, sport team jackets, and athletic socks.
- Jeans.
- Shorts and capris.

5. Study the list of don'ts. Avoid the following items, which, fortunately or unfortunately, don't fall under the category of business casual:

- Sneakers, sandals, flip-flops or other open-toed shoes.
- Sports shirts, sweatshirts, sport team jackets, and athletic socks.
- Shorts and capris.
- Jeans.
- Very tight, and hence revealing, cuts of pants. No skinny-trousers allowed.

Permissions

Index

A
Active Listening, 15, 48-49
Attitude, 1, 16, 19, 21, 28, 35, 50, 164

B
Basic Etiquette, 35, 125, 130
Basic Table Manners, 124, 131, 138
Behave Professionally, 90, 125
Body Language, 35, 77, 90, 125, 127
Body Odor, 113, 115-118
Business Casual, 88, 164, 166, 170, 174-177, 182-184, 186-188
Business Etiquette, 1, 3-4, 6, 35, 66
Business Lunch, 126-127, 129, 139
Business Meal, 125-126, 128-129, 132, 138
Business Meeting Etiquette, 3, 87
Business Talk, 4, 128-129

C
Chew with your Mouth Closed, 124, 132, 156
Clean Up After Yourself, 122, 124
Common Hygiene Mistakes, 101, 110, 112
Communication Etiquette, 35
Company Protocol, 124
Corporate Dressing, 164-165
Cough and Sneeze Etiquette, 101, 109
Coworker, 6, 9, 11, 13, 75, 78
Cubicle Space, 10

D
Deadline, 33
Dining Etiquette, 3, 137
Dress Appropriately, 6, 89, 126
Dress Code, 2, 6, 88, 164-167, 171, 180, 182

E
Eating Etiquette, 124
Electronics Etiquette, 4
Email Etiquette, 3, 36, 75, 79
Employee Handbook, 53, 124, 183

F
Fellow Employee, 20, 22

G
Good Employee, 19-20
Good Etiquette, 2, 12, 93
Good Hygiene, 115, 125
Good Worker, 18-19

H
Hygiene Etiquettes, 101

I
Instant Messaging Etiquette, 94

M
Meeting Etiquette, 3, 87

N
New Employee, 23, 29

O
Office Environment, 12, 138
Office Gossip, 9, 30

P
Personal Grooming, 12, 117, 119
Personal Hygiene, 5, 112, 116, 119, 169
Phone Etiquette, 36, 46, 56
Picking Up the Phone, 41, 68, 73
Professional Courtesy, 3, 29
Professional Greeting, 2, 46, 56-57
Professional Image, 41, 164
Professional Language, 66, 76
Professionalism, 2, 24, 53, 56, 101, 165
Punctuality, 30-31

S
Scheduling, 30-31
Shared Space Etiquette, 5
Smelly Food, 125, 138

T
Table Manners, 124, 131-132, 138
Talking on the Phone, 37, 43, 62, 64-65
Telephone Etiquette, 35, 62, 67-68

W

Work Environment, 21, 166
Work Goals, 19, 21
Workplace Appropriate, 8, 55

Workplace Communication Etiquettes, 35
Written Communication, 36

Printed in the USA
CPSIA information can be obtained
at www.ICGtesting.com
JSHW051622061123
51533JS00005B/69